Awa

Your Ultimate Spiritual Journey

Brett Jones

Enlightened Publications

First published in 2015 by

Enlightened Publications
PO Box 906
Canning Bridge, Perth WA 6000

National Library of Australia
Cataloguing-in-Publication entry

Creator: Jones, Brett, 1958- author.

Title: Awaken : your ultimate spiritual journey/Brett Jones.

ISBN: 9780646936482 (paperback)

Subjects: Spirituality.

Consciousness--Religious aspects.

Enlightenment.

Ego (Psychology)--Religious aspects.

Dewey Number: 204.2

Also by Brett Jones

Winds of Change

The Forgotten Secrets of Lasting Forever

Table of Contents

On seeing Buddha, [Dona] went to him and said, "Master,
are you a deva [a god]?"
"No, brahman, I am not a deva."
"… a yakkha [a kind of protector god, or sometimes a
trickster spirit]?"
"No…"
"… a human being?"
"No, brahman, I am not a human being."
"Then what sort of being are you?"
"Remember me, brahman, as
'awakened'."(1)

PRELUDE

In human history, we have never been richer, had more, created more, nor inspired greater technological advances. Yet we have never been so unhappy.

The World Happiness Report (2013) shows people in developed regions such as Europe, North America, Australia/New Zealand are less happy than they were in 2005 – despite increased economic wealth.(2) The Happy Planet Index (2014) shows that countries such as Indonesia are happier than any developed nation.(3) Indeed, the top 10 nations on the happiness index are all developing nations. It is all too obvious from these studies that wealth and riches bring neither happiness nor fulfilment.

There needs to be a change in how we perceive life and what we want from it. If following our current path of ongoing economic development in a bid to achieve personal and national happiness is not working, then what would work? What path can we follow? And how do we find it?

Throughout human history there have been teachers of consciousness who have led many to a higher level of happiness than most of us will ever experience, because most of what we seek is transitory. It does not last. Success in business is temporary and disappears when we die. A triumph on the sporting field lasts just a moment, the focus turning quickly to the next game or the next season. A relationship can be wonderful one moment and disastrous the next. Children grow and leave. A beautiful sunset fades. A blooming flower dies.

To find a higher level of consciousness requires you to step away from what you think you know and allow yourself to experience what is not available in the normal world of consciousness.

If you open your eyes, you will find the majority of the world is asleep – their consciousness runs on autopilot. Some people rise, have a shower, eat breakfast, dress and fall out the door into the car or onto the bus and go through the day with no thought of what they are doing or why. They are unaware and asleep. This is the sad reality.

If you wish to seek true happiness, there is only one place, one part of the universe, which is constant. That is the consciousness inside you. This may seem unfamiliar to some, but if you are ready, the idea of rediscovering your consciousness will strike a note that holds true for you. You will know you want to *awaken*. If you do not, you are still under the influence of the one thing that creates the unhappiness that you experience every day.

You do not know this thing that influences you because it casts a mirror that makes it appear as if the external world is at fault. If only your job would be less demanding, if your son or daughter would obey you, if that beloved person would return your love, if only problems would stop, if money would start to flow – then you would be happy. It appears certain to you that the root of your unhappiness is caused by factors outside of yourself.

This is the delusion.

The true cause of your unhappiness and your suffering is within the part of you that makes the choices that places you in these situations to begin with. This part of you does not want you to *awaken* or know the joy that every moment of life can bring. Learning to discover, understand and know this part of you is the first step to *awaken*.

This part of you is the ego. So, to begin, you must recognise your ego, because to be free and live the life you were born to, to become enlightened, you must know this part of yourself. Your journey demands this.

Many of us do not even know it exists and have never really experienced freedom from it. Describing your consciousness is like describing a beautiful desert island with sparkling turquoise waters and plentiful fish to a nomadic desert dweller. It may sound wonderful, but they have no concept of what it is really like. *Awakening* can be the key to unlocking that awareness in you.

Living without the ego is pure joy. No matter what happens, your life can be one that holds no stress, fear or anxiety. This is not controlled by will, it simply does not arise. It is freedom from suffering.

Life becomes a dance, a dance of knowing yourself fully, of receiving what you deserve, and a mystical journey that now calms the mind and heart. Living from your true nature, you will love like you never have before. Life holds no fear anymore because you know the truth. Life is seen for what it really is, an experience of no suffering. How can it be possible to suffer when nothing unreal can threaten you?

The old way of living is dying. Abuse inspired by the ego of ourselves, our political system, of the very planet that gives us life is making us unhappy, and we are becoming aware that unhappiness grows. There is also awareness that what we are doing is not working in our daily lives. Many of us are seeking more. We are seeking to *awaken*. We are all on a journey in life. That journey can be along a road that takes us to the forest or it can be climbing a mountain and standing on top to see the view.

To *awaken* is to see clearly and come home to the divine in you. This is your ultimate journey. When you take this journey is up to you. That you will is certain.

Awaken describes the condition we all find ourselves in when we are trapped by the ego. The ego is covered in detail in the Introduction and the first chapter. In the second chapter we look at how to *awaken* in a practical day-to-day sense, while the final chapter embraces more in-depth teachings on how to *awaken*. This will also introduce you to a new method of meditation called rapid induction meditation (RIM) and how to quickly move into deep states of connection.

These teachings are not for monks, who are able to devote their entire existence to enlightenment. They are for advanced souls who can identify their ego and take no offence when it is pointed out, because they know it is not their true self but have not yet found how to separate and be free from it.

The 8000-year-old *Tao Te Ching* expresses it beautifully:

> *When a superior man heard of Tao,*
> *He cultivates himself diligently.*
> *When an average man heard of Tao,*
> *He is doubtful, vague and would give up halfway.*
> *When an inferior man heard of Tao,*
> *He laughs and thinks of it as foolish.*(4)

Awaken is a guide to the practices that will enable *awakening* in the only way that is possible – through a journey to know what the divine is through personal experience. The divine is consciousness, the underlying awareness that exists in everything in this universe.

Awaken is not a theoretical work. It is based on observable truths available to every person who lives on this planet. It points to truths from every religion, and from science, and shows how they all fit together to reveal that we are all on the same path to discover why we are here. It is also designed to help you know for certain that you are constantly called to this purpose by the divine. That you are loved beyond measure and that you are always safe and cared for. *Awaken* will show you how to connect and remain connected to the divine. This is an experience confirming who you are, not a belief system to adopt.

The more you seek to know yourself and the truth of who you are and, conversely, the influence of the one thing that causes your suffering – the ego – the more you will *awaken*.

INTRODUCTION

The ego

The ego identifies with the body.

It loves it.

The ego dresses it up, promotes it, adores it, puts makeup on it and tries in any way it can to make it better than it is. Botox, plastic surgery, breast enhancements, hair replacements.

The ego thinks that it is the body. It thinks that it must keep the body alive and make it look better than it is. That's why it loves tattoos, ear piercings, expensive watches, and air-brushed photos. That's why it wants to freeze your body and bring you back in the future. That's why it wants to download your brain and put it into a robot so that you can live forever.

Anything that adds or builds the ego. This is the basic dilemma for the ego is: it's never enough.

The ego came into existence in you, the moment that you came into this world. The ego was already here as a collective mindset and energy which was adopted when you were born. You plugged into the delusion.

At that precise time you forgot who you were and became aware of who you think you are. You temporarily separated from your own consciousness and became aware of the false self that you created, and then continued to build this self. You gave the personal ego life and, like any form of life in this universe, it wants to continue to live and will fight to do so.

The ego has a life of its own. It thinks and creates thought on its own.

Consider this. If you took a moment to stop your busy thinking pattern, you would realize that the ego generates its own thoughts. It's always commenting on you and others – in fact, everything. It's always comparing, always keeping itself alive by getting you to satisfy its insatiable hunger for negative thought, which becomes negative energy.

Buddhists call it monkey mind. It never stops; it is always active, always speaking. To have freedom from the ego, you must come to awareness and realize it controls you. Lao Tzu and Buddha experienced such enlightenment. Christ realized that he had the power not to listen. Buddha was tempted on the night of his enlightenment by Mara, and Jesus in the desert by the devil.

The young Prince Siddhartha, as Buddha was called before enlightenment, left his palace for a life of asceticism in order to experience, what he called, the cessation of suffering. He left behind his wife and young son to wander the forest and observe ascetic practices for six years. He practiced to the point of death – he could feel his spine through his stomach – one day realizing that these extreme practices were not drawing him closer to his goal.

He traveled on to a grove and sat beneath a Bodhi tree, vowing he would not move until he became enlightened and found the way to the cessation of suffering for all. That night, according to legend, he passed through three levels of insight: past lives, the laws of karma, and lastly freedom from Mara, or the laws of attachment. Later that night, he recounted that he was tempted by Mara, the manifestation of the force of the ego.

He resisted everything that it offered him. Finally, it gave up. He then saw clearly how the universe was created and how the many worlds were in fact one. The story, in its explanation of reality, is very similar to that of the *Samithas*, an ancient Hindu text nearly 4000 years old.

The story of Jesus in his 40-day and 40-night fast in the desert, also tells of the devil tempting him with food, power and faith. His task was to ignore these temptations and focus on the truth, staying the course to realize his true purpose. The task is always the same; the story of achieving it too.

These two teachers and many others throughout history have passed on the same teachings, expressed in different ways through different cultural lenses, but only the one truth. The truth of who we are, how we came to be here and what our purpose is.

Unfortunately, that truth has been distorted by the reality we live in, and is filtered through the one thing that holds us in delusion.

The modern word for this is ego. You have it in you and it is the cause of your suffering. The ego is the negative part of this universe and it exists in all of us. It is the part of you that criticises yourself, or projects blame for what goes wrong onto others. It is the part of you that you hear in your head arguing with you about whether you should do something or not. It is the part of you that makes you sad, angry, lonely, depressed, anxious or unhappy. It is the part of you that you believe is you but it's not. It has a life of its own.

The ego attempts to hide the truth from you. The truth of who you are and the truth of why the universe exists. The truth of your real life. A truth that becomes clear when you *awaken*.

The words in this book are inadequate to fully express the experience of being at one with the force of that truth. Words are a poor exchange for an experience that must be felt to be fully comprehended, and that is the basis of wisdom.

Words may fail to fully convey with precision what true experience and wisdom bring to the truth. They are merely fingers pointing to the truth.

Buddha realized that the root cause of everything is suffering and he attempted to explain that this realization involves a change of consciousness from the unconscious to the conscious. You cannot understand consciousness with unconsciousness. You can only move to a place where consciousness exists and experience it from there. You cannot experience it with the ego in the way.

What these teachings offer will only be of interest to you if you have reached a point in your journey where you are ready to be *awakened* to the real cause of why you are here and are an advanced soul who is open to the truth. Many, unfortunately, are not ready and will stay in delusion for a while longer.

Writings in the past have attempted to convey that which cannot be understood, only experienced. Allow your heart to feel the truth of the words contained in *Awaken* rather than understand them with the mind.

The message in this book has been sent to you by many people from many different historical periods: by Buddha, Marcus Aurelius, Shakespeare and Aristotle, movies such as *The Matrix*, and sacred scriptures such as the Bible, the Upanishads, the Koran and the Vedic texts.

At some point in your journey you will *awaken* to the light that you are and the light that lives in us all. This book may be that *awakening* for you. I pray that it is.

In the beginning ...

There was no form and then form came into existence. It had *awakened*.

The Heavens and the Earth were created.

You are form and you are part of the universe, and as part of it you are bound by its rules. One of them is Death.

The ego is frightened of Death.

It fears it because it believes that death is the end and so it fears what it thinks is real. It has no concept of anything beyond death.

One of the traps the ego uses to keep you bound to it is to give you understanding. If you were raised in a religious tradition, you will have knowledge that there is life after death. That knowledge, though, doesn't impact on how you react to or perceive the world. It's a theory, an idea, a concept, but it's not believed at the heart level; it's not real to you as an experience.

You are shaped and influenced by experience, for better or for worse, and spiritually it is through experience that you will find freedom, the divine or enlightenment, whatever you wish to call it.

When something happens in your day, it is not the event that happens that matters, but how you react to it. From that reaction, outcomes occur or do not occur for you. You are not free to react as you choose. The ego will always be there to interpret events: "She did that to me because she hates me"; "He ignored me because he is a bad person. He is always undervaluing me." And so it goes on. You believe what it says and you react to it. The frame through which you look at the world is the ego and you have to remove the frame to see the world as it is.

Anything else is delusion, delusion of the ego. Most people live in that delusion, though this is now slowly changing.

The knowledge that there is life after death is perceived through this frame of denying death and trying to avoid it. It is a belief that is adopted but not experienced as a truth of our existence.

The ego avoids death by denying it is ever going to happen. As ridiculous as this sounds, it is true. Anyone who smokes is in complete denial of death. An obese person overeating is in complete denial of death. The ego's greatest weapon is denial. It can fool you into thinking anything – if you are not aware.

The ego is about delusion and hiding the truth from you.

So the ego doesn't believe that you have consciousness that is the same nature as that of the divine and that consciousness will live on forever. The ego can't believe that, as its only belief is in death.

This truth was spoken of by Buddha during the night of his enlightenment and can be experienced directly by you as you also *awaken*. It is not a theory or belief to be adopted. Experience is what counts. That is the cornerstone of truth.

It is pointless learning mindfulness or meditation if you have not experienced the truth. This is like reading all the books on driving a car, then sitting in it and starting the engine, but being too fearful to take your foot off the brake.

The truth is you will not *awaken* until you learn the teachings and reach awareness of who you really are and become one again with your true nature. The ego cannot accept this because it means it will die. Once it dies, there will be no need for form. The darkness will disappear and there will be perfection, a return to the divine.

In the universe, there is more dark matter than light, (5) but eventually that balance will change. That is what you are here to do unless you become lost in the delusion of birth and death of which the Buddha spoke.

The Tao Te Ching, written by Lao Tzu in China over 8000 years ago, spoke of death in this way.

> *By knowing the creation of all lives, one can then return to the origin and abide by the Mother.*
> *It is in this way that although the body dies, the spiritual nature will not perish.*(4)

Sixty-eight percent of the universe is so-called dark energy, and 25 percent is dark matter. The matter that we can see actually makes up less than 5 percent of the universe.(5) Gravity and dark energy are at this time scientifically inexplicable, but are thought to be causing expansion of the universe. There is no unified theory that explains everything. That is because we cannot use the very thing that created it, the mind, to explain it.

Yet you use your mind every day to interpret the universe you live in. You use it to make decisions based on data that is fed into it by your senses – data that the ego distorts and bends to suit its view of the world.

Regardless of culture, race or religion, the ego rules. It pervades every country, every political party, most political decisions. It values form, and most decisions are made on form. Let's build more schools and educate more people so we can build more stuff to sell that we don't really need and don't really want. Let's pollute the planet so that eventually the ego will kill it.

The ego's influence also pervades most mainstream media, resulting in a focus on the negative of life rather than the positive. Featuring crime, as opposed to creativity.

The ego has common thought patterns that infiltrate every person. It actually wants you dead. In its madness, it is prepared to kill its host. The thinking goes "I'm suffering so much, I'm better off dead." That thought pattern is expressed in its extreme in suicide. Equally, it is expressed in the slow death of the smoker or in the world's economic engine running rampant with no thought for our planet's health.

It will only be different when we all finally *awaken* to realize that we are immortal, eternal and do live forever. When that frame becomes real for you, you will act differently, think differently and want different things for all those around you. You will know that they are you and you are they and all travelling the same journey together.

The Tao illuminates this principle.

> *Human(s) must achieve the ultimate void and maintain calmness with sincerity in order to observe the growth and flourish of all beings.*
> *It is in this way that one can understand the law of nature.*
> *All things and beings will eventually return to the original source.*

This is called "peace".
"Peace" means returning to one's original nature.
This original nature is the eternal law. To know the
nature's law is to be enlightened.(4)

A Course in Miracles says:

Nothing real can be threatened, nothing unreal
exists.(6)

This means that your true nature can never be harmed and that the ego is a delusion and does not really exist. It also refers to all that the ego has created as not being real. Your true nature is what is real and it can never be threatened. It has been called by many names, but I will call it the divine.

The insanity of the ego knows no bounds. It manifests its self from an early age in our culture and how we raise our children. We teach them that the separation is real. "You must achieve, you must compete." "Believe in doing the right thing but lie at times." "Do your best but always be better than everyone else." "If someone is mean to you, then you'd better get them back." These cultural norms are all forms of separation that are ego inspired.

What if you broke away from the norm and suggested to your children that they have an ego and it talks to them and tells them things that are not true? What if they could be raised to know they are immortal and that in this life they are being led by signs from the divine that exist all around them on what they should be doing and why. That could be the start of a new way of experiencing life for them.

Awakening

When I was small I had no concept of the ego or what it was. I was raised a Catholic and went to Catholic schools where I was taught the then concepts that God was good and I was evil and tainted by Original Sin, and that I was damned to hell if I didn't go to church on a Sunday. These concepts now seem as intelligent as the Mayan rituals of human sacrifice to appease the gods. Church quickly lost its appeal.

By my teens I had, like most others, worked out that religion wasn't making much sense. The preached statements about God being love but at the same time threatening to send us to hell didn't jell. The obvious question which no one seemed to be able to answer was, "Why would the divine send his only son to earth to tell us what we needed to do. Why didn't he just heal us?" The more I learnt about the early history of the Catholic church, such as the filtering of the story and the discarding of the agnostic gospels of Thomas, Judas, Mary and others, the more I became disillusioned. Other facts like the New Testament Gospels being written 50–100 years after his death by authors who had never met Jesus raised more doubts and questions about the accuracy and interpretation of the words. This questioning of, and insight into, the development of the religion eventually led me to awareness. God became a distant concept.

After school, it seemed obligatory to follow everyone else and become successful, so I built a career in real estate. I was very good at it and by age 24 had left a real estate agency to start my own development company; by age 27 I had built numerous buildings valued in the hundreds of millions. What became apparent, though, was the lack of fulfilment I experienced in my life despite this success and wealth. Interestingly, many others on similar life paths have experienced the same.

By age 30 I had lost most of the wealth. My last few dollars were spent on a car to carry my, then, four children around.

It was at that point a friend suggested a course that may help not only my failing marriage but also myself.

I wasn't aware at the time, but I had what can only be described as a spiritual *awakening*. Even though it wasn't a religious course, I experienced a profound, undeniable connection to what is real, a connection to the divine in myself.

For months afterwards, I felt calm and at peace, and the way in which I reacted to the world had changed. What occurred on the outside didn't disturb the peace I felt on the inside. That feeling, however, changed as time went by; it wasn't yet permanent, but a transformation had certainly happened. I was at times sucked back into the ego and believed what it said to me. It allowed others to pull me from the peace for brief periods. However, the underlying awareness and sense of peace did not change.

I was fortunate shortly after to travel on a yacht with my wife, Marie, for three years. This trip was an important milestone, allowing me to discover peace and solitude and the truth about my own life. Thousands of miles from anywhere with only my own thoughts and the sounds of the wind and the ocean was a profound way to experience the divine inside me and in the world around me.

This experience was a part of my journey to reach the truth.

During my search I read thousands of books on spirituality to understand what had happened to me, what they were saying and what they meant. The more religions I studied, the more the obvious became clear. They were all saying the same thing, just in different ways. However, it still took many years to realize that understanding something and knowing it are entirely different, the latter involving direct experience of the divine.

Then I discovered letting go and trusting, and soon the insights I had experienced opened a new way of being in the world. This led to a new way of meditating to reach the divine more directly. I had *awoken*.

God as a word has too many negative connotations. I prefer, now, to use the word divine to describe the central one, the singularity that is all consciousness, all love and all life. Its consciousness and yours are one and the same.

If you seek the same journey, then at some point you must be open to grace touching your life. If you are, you will be blessed with an opening, a moment to experience something that will transform your life. As I discovered, preparation provides the fertile soil for it to take seed, but preparation does not mean understanding.

Understanding is what the ego is constantly doing. It is always comparing, always seeking someone or something new to understand and judge. Knowing comes from what is true in you, the part of you that is your consciousness and is immortal, and just knows what you should do. It is your soul. Knowing is an experience.

Being connected to your consciousness is what some people call intuition, but when most say they have intuition, it is from an egoic point of view – as if it's some special talent or gift. The truth is: it's who you really are. Every single one of you. You have the ability to find the truth right now and connect with the divine.

Understanding the ego is only important as a means to free yourself from it – to *awaken*. It is like trying to describe the ocean to a fish in a pond. It has no concept of what it is. All it knows is the pond, and it likes the pond, even though the ocean is larger and more beautiful.

You live in the ego and prefer it simply because that is all you know. I know inside that I, like all of you, can help many others to *awaken* to the truth.

I have learnt that understanding and having all the knowledge in the world will not assist you to *awaken*. It is like the mechanic who builds a car and then stands proudly looking at the completed vehicle, only to hear the buyer say, "But where is the engine?" The car looks great but it has no power to it. So, too, are many lives that are built for show, not substance.

You cannot *awaken* until all the groundwork is done. That involves personal insight and not being led further into delusion by the ego. It is truly only in experience that you can know the truth.

At times you will wander into the egoic mind and be lost, but that is all part of the journey. Do not give up.

These words I'm writing may be just words read by you, or they may be an experience and felt through your heart as an *awakening*, which becomes an experience and, in that experience, a truth comes to life for you. As you read, seek inside how this relates to you. Not because I say it is the truth, or anyone else does, but because you come to know for yourself that it is true and is likewise for every single person in the world.

I have spent the last two decades teaching and helping others to become *awakened*. Teaching how to live in this egoic world as part of it, but removed from its effects. So I know many of the questions that you would like to ask of me to find your own way to the truth.

The Tao says:

> *One who knows other people is wise.*
> *One who knows himself (themselves) is enlightened.*(4)

The teachings that follow outline a practice and method of reaching the divine and the truth. The questions posed are those that have been asked by many seekers of the truth. My responses do not come from me personally, but as a conduit for the same message that is sent to you every day in millions of ways. This is nothing special, as you are all able to do this. The ego, of course, tries to make it something special, that only some can do. Nothing is further from the truth.

The first lesson is to repeat the Buddha's words:

... this is my way, each of you will find your own. There are many paths to the same place. This is but one.(1)

Chapter 1

THE TEACHINGS

What is the ego?

It is the Tao Yin, Hindu Shiva, the Judaic devil, the Egyptian Apep, the Buddhist Mara. It is the negative force in the universe, the force of destruction. In Taoism the universe is a duality. There is black and white, hot and cold, and so on. Hence in us there is good and evil, understanding and ignorance, peace and war, love and fear. The ego is the opposite of the truth.

For everything you truly are, the ego is the opposite.

You connect to the ego from the moment you come back into this universe. You can see it in the muscle structure on the left side of your face. Look at most photos, the eye and the muscle structure is different on that side. There is a shadow behind the eye – you can sense it, you can see it. It exists physically in you as well as speaking to you in your mind.

The Tao Te Ching explains it as:

> *All beings bear the negative physical form which is represented by Ying, and embrace the positive true nature which is represented by Yang.*

With the union of these two, they arrive at a state of harmony.(4)

To *awaken* you must balance the two forces inside yourself. You must know the ego and know the divine. Not as knowledge but as experience.

In the universe, all creative force is the divine and all destructive force is the ego. Inside you, the creative force is expressed for one purpose, to return home. The ego, on the other hand, is the destructive force and seeks one thing: to keep itself alive by keeping you in delusion and separating you from your connection to the divine. It has numerous ways of achieving this, as the teachings will show.

The ego will lie to you. It will not stop talking. In it, there is no peace. Conversely, your truth always comes with a feeling of what is the right thing to do. The words in your head are always from your ego. The ego speaks words, your truth feels right. In deeper states of meditation, truth has clarity, in contrast to the frantic energy and confusion of the veil the ego raises to keep you from connecting to the divine.

The ego is split between the collective ego that runs through everyone and your personal one, which is the storage of all your negative experiences. The collective ego is the central delusion that our souls are not immortal and will die into nothing. This collective ego can lead nations into delusion, as in Nazi Germany, Rwanda or Cambodia under Pol Pot. The collective ego is about separation, deluding you that you are all different, pushing you to see that those differences are not to be trusted, they must in fact be killed: "These people are not like me." This to the ego can be in the colour of your skin, your religious belief, your nationality, because to the ego it doesn't really matter. The collective ego has been behind some of humanity's greatest wars and genocides.

The personal ego is different; it stores all your personal events. They are recorded and placed into an area of your brain that has no access to the positive experiences of your life. So, when it works out a strategy for solving problems, the ego will say this is how it's done and this will generally lead you to exactly what you don't want. That's why you keep running into the same boyfriend or girlfriend, the same marriage, or the same boss or job.

These are called patterns, and the ego stores and controls them.

You may have experienced your intimate partner hurting you when all you want is to be loved. So, based on past experiences, the ego says the solution is not to open your heart to them. The result of course is that they will close off as well when they feel you closing off. So now you receive less love.

This is not an intelligent way to respond, but the ego will use your fear of being hurt to power you into responding the same way each time until eventually you divorce and have to find another person with whom to practise this lesson.

You all know you have two voices in your head that seem at times in conflict. One of these is not your true self. This is a misconception born from the ego to mislead you. Jesus said, "I am always with you", meaning the divine, your consciousness, is always there. It's inside you but not in the voices in your head; they will always be your ego.

Jesus's statement, "I am the way, the truth, and the life: no man cometh unto the Father, but by me", wasn't a statement about himself, it was about the divine inside him and you. The "me" is your own divine speaking through him. The Buddha spoke of the piercing of Mara on the night of his enlightenment. In the second watch of the night he saw how "beings vanish and come to be again". Only in the clarity of that consciousness experience can this knowledge be known as the truth.

That is what you seek. Having knowledge about, or even believing, isn't the same as the experience of it and therefore the knowing of it. Many believe they are consciousness but few really know it by experience.

As you become aware, the practice of understanding that every judgment, every voice you hear in your mind, is your ego can be difficult. It is, however, a great practice. Buddha called it "monkey mind", always jumping from one thought to the next, never happy to rest, always creating thought. Its purpose is to hide what is right there in front of you.

The ego is always using itself as the filter of what you see, hear and experience. A glass is never a glass. You like or dislike its shape. The taste of the water may be different from what you are used to, the water temperature may be too cold. You never just experience the glass.

The ego does this with everything by removing you from the moment. It has a comment or opinion on everything. It never rests and it never stops. Practising mindfulness can assist in giving discipline to your practice. Mindfulness, however, is just a tool, not an end in itself.

Sit still for one moment and attempt not to think. It's almost impossible, isn't it? Very quickly, a thought will pop in to your mind. The more you practise, though, the more you will find you are able to sit quietly without a thought being real to you. But if you lose focus, suddenly you will find yourself swept away in a wave of thought that consumes you and pulls you from reality.

At a lower level of energy or vibration, you will act on that thought and believe it is you who had the thought.

Moving to *awaken* you will be clear it is not you. Clarity of thought comes, as well as clarity of heart and clarity of emotions, which lead ultimately to connection with the divine. You can decide what you wish to feel and how you wish to react.

That is when you *awaken*.

How much does the ego affect me?

In every moment the ego is present and the only remedy is to be aware of its influence. If you become self aware, you will hear it comment and offer an opinion on everything that occurs around you.

It is the constant companion of anyone with consciousness and is the opposite of consciousness. It lives in delusion and seeks to have us live in the same place with it. The sad truth is that the majority of us do.

So, many of us fail to remain conscious to how it affects our decisions. It will tell us a story of our life and why we do what we do. "That's just me" it says to justify our anger, our laziness, our lust or our avarice.

It tells a story of subtlety. One we can believe because, if the story was too violent or too critical, it would never convince us. So it starts slowly: "You are not good at this or that." Then it comments on other people: "Look at them, they are fat or stupid or arrogant or rich." Slowly it turns your view of the world around, affecting how you feel every day about life.

Equally, do not think that if you do not identify with these harsher forms of the ego they don't affect you. The ego can drain you of your soul and your energy by making you work hard to save others, to assist them, to exhaust yourself for your children because "that is the right thing to do". If you don't, then you will experience guilt, the emotion that is the bane of every mother's life.

The ego will justify you overeating, smoking, spending time running or cycling when you should be spending time with your family, staying silent when you should speak up. It can easily make you think that you are justified in what you do.

It will be subtle with you. It may make you irritable and not pleasant to be around so that people may refer to you as Mr. Grumpy. Even if you have accumulated wealth and position and built professional standing in life, you will still be subject to the ego's ways. It will make you feel superior, which will manifest in the tone in your voice, the tilt of your head, the look down under your glasses. But if you pause and have a moment of awareness, you will notice that those you love feel they cannot reach you. They may attempt to, but the wall of superiority may hold them back.

The voice in your head says, "It's just them anyway. So they have problems, they need to deal with them. You get on with most people." However, what the ego blinds you to is that if you lose your position and wealth those so-called friends you get on with will disappear. Then you will come face to face with what the ego has hidden. It is you who has the problem. It is called delusion.

Perhaps you have spent your life devoted to helping others, working hard to be of service to the divine, doing more than most and feeling you are on the right path. The ego welcomes you too. It can still use what you have learned to convince you that you are a good person, not like those others still lost and seeking the divine. This is just another form of superiority, and another judgment by the ego. It is always judging, no matter how subtly, and judgment is another form of separation.

Separation is the ego's principle weapon. The truth is "they" are "you" in the next life. The ego doesn't believe this, it is only concerned with this body you are in right now, and it is convinced this is what must survive because to it that is all that is real. The ego is never on the same level as another person; it always places your self-image above others or below others. This is its principle form of separation. It then further separates on race, creed, intelligence and wealth.

You may observe yourself or others losing faith and hope and their lives going off track. These situations are all due to the ego. You may undergo psychotherapy and tame the ego into being quiet, but ultimately it will return to you, albeit in a more subtle form because now with increased awareness you will not believe the ego as you did before. However, it will still run your life.

The ego uses everything for two basic purposes: to make a goal of all things in your life, and to separate. The ego can make a goal for enlightenment, raising a child, making money, growing lawn. Its objective is to create a meaning for your existence in what is essentially a meaningless universe. It seeks distraction for you in order to take your focus and concentration away from the truth, to amuse yourself whilst you are here and in that way keep itself alive. Its strategy is distraction.

It also seeks to separate and in doing so keep your energy from coming together with everyone else's. It will use race, intelligence, competition, anything to separate. Your seemingly separate bodies, lives that appear disconnected. This, however, is not the truth as you are all connected and the moments of connection are present all the time if you could but see them. That chance meeting is the divine at work in a reality that it cannot change because it is your will that will not be changed and it would not go against your will.

A chance meeting or a song on the radio at the right moment is a moment of *awakening* or it is simply an ego-based moment of nothing. Use it in the right way and you can bring *awakening*, that moment holding a clue to what you should do. Freud called it synchronicity. Some call it the butterfly principle. Both mean what you do affects all others.

In synchronicity you move closer to the divine through moments of clarity. One event or moment leads to another where you can find the easiest path to your ultimate purpose.

The truth, however, is that the divine is in you, and when you recognize it and identify fully with it, you will be free. The ego will have no hold and you will experience the true joy of life.

How does the Ego reel us in? How does this process begin?

Being born into this universe, you are immediately part of form and subject to its rules and laws. One is that the ego has an energy to it that affects everything. It is the Yang of the Tao. It is the force of destruction that is evident in nature.

The same force that causes the wind to erode a mountain, a leaf to die, a sun to explode is the force in you that slowly erodes at your will.

Being part of this universe, you have Yin and Yang, the duality of life and all things, in you, including this destructive element which begins to learn about life through you. Something will happen when you are young through one of four influencers: a family member, an event, school, or your peer group. Perhaps your father passes early, a child pushes you in the playground, someone abuses you. Something happens to everyone. This event, whatever it may be, has an emotional impact. Your ego wants to interpret it and it says it will keep you safe, and in this way it gives meaning to the event. Then it creates a pattern to follow for all similar events.

"Dad passed away because the doctors couldn't save him," the ego concludes. So now the ego decides that doctors can't be trusted, and for the rest of your life, your ego will not trust any doctor.

The ego takes one belief and applies it to all things. It makes the one event a global belief.

Someone abuses you. Now the ego concludes not just that one person can't be trusted but all people can't be trusted. So for the rest of your life you can't trust anyone. You won't let them close to you, and this affects your relationships, your business, your accumulation of wealth.

What was once an event now has become a pattern that is repeated many times. When you begin to examine your life from that perspective, you can see how this pattern arose.

It is not the event that causes harm. The event is merely an experience. It is the ego creating a mental construct of meaning about the event that causes damage. The mental construct holds the vibration, or pain, in place and uses it as the fuel to keep the pattern alive. The event is stored in the subconscious with the pain. The ego then uses this to run the pattern to avoid the pain. It does avoid it, but creates a far higher level of pain than the pain it sought to avoid.

If you have suffered physical abuse, the ego will either turn it into a pattern, causing other people around you to suffer from the physical abuse you in turn impose on them, or suppress it, resulting in depression or your feeling isolated or different and closed off from others.

If your father smacked you, your ego will have you beat your own children. "They need a good smack," it will say, "nothing wrong with a good smack. I got hit, there's nothing wrong with me." It perpetuates the destruction of your child's self-esteem. It controls your actions at a lower level of unconsciousness, where you react to things rather than have choice over your reactions. It will not allow you to pause to consider what effect this has on your child and what pattern it now sets in place for them.

The second delusion is that the ego must keep you occupied and not focused on reality. It will ensure you have no peace. It will create drama in your life. It achieves this because it always has an expectation about the future and what *should* happen. It has rules about your life based on its belief that life is predictable.

When one of those rules is broken, the ego will fire into action: judging, blaming, defending itself against attack. It will use anger or annoyance or many other myriad emotions to project the "error" in its plan on to someone else. If you were expecting your wife or husband to do something and they didn't, watch as the ego ignites and tells them why it should have been done.

The ego also keeps us occupied. Most of us drive with the radio on and come home and immediately switch it on again, or turn the TV on. We prefer this to the silence in our minds, which would be immediately filled with the ego's incessant voice. What we fail to realize is the silence under the ego's voice is our freedom from it.

The ego attempts to keep us thinking – always.

This process appears inescapable. Yet it can be, by beginning to dismantle the delusion that these patterns are built on – in other words, to *awaken*.

Once they are brought into awareness, the patterns collapse. Once the truth of the delusion can be seen, it has no power. The original decision that created the patterns is seen as a lie.

When the dad passed, it may have been that he was very ill and the doctors did their best to save him, but it was just his time. Seen from that reality the pattern collapses.

The truth now seen fulfils the saying, "The truth will set you free."

Why do we listen to the ego at all?

The technique the ego uses is simple.

The ego is seeking to keep you focused on the world in front of you. That's what Jesus meant when he said:

> *Do you not know that friendship with the world is hostility toward God? Therefore whoever wishes to be a friend of the world makes himself an enemy of God.(7)*

He knew the ego is always seeking to draw you into a false reality based on what you experienced in the past. This is not reality, it is delusion. There is a greater truth available that the ego does not want you to see.

It is insistent and always speaking. It will pop thoughts into your head constantly. Become aware, observe. One moment you are thinking about something, then a random thought pops into your head. You don't consider where it came from and the next moment you are angry because it mentioned someone that may have done wrong by you. It had nothing to do with what you were thinking about, but now you are upset and focused on the anger, through which the ego has taken control of you.

You listen then, because what it says appears to be the "truth". It is, however, only the ego's version of the truth. It uses one "truth" and then another until it convinces you that it is you and you must only trust its voice. From that point it becomes the only voice you can hear.

Until you can find a new way of seeing the world, you will continue to believe the lies the ego creates. Whilst you are in its trance, you will truly believe that these are the truth because they feel and appear to be that way. This is the delusion in which the ego holds you.

The ego will also provide an identity for you to hold on to as another form of separation from others and from the truth of who you are. It may make you into a doctor or a successful business person, a soldier, a biker, criminal or star. Any of these illusions are the ego's attempt at separation. The ego will use it to make you feel superior or inferior to others. It will use it so that you cannot feel yourself residing in your body. You will be too busy projecting the false image on to others, modifying what you say, how you say it, the way you dress, the way you look to conform to the image.

If people do not respect the image, then the ego will modify the image or do harm to those who do not give the ego the respect it feels it deserves. This method works well in your personal ego as well as the collective ego. It is frequently the basis of wars between countries.

Your version of the ego may be different in its techniques or strategies; however, it will still hold you in mild dissatisfaction. You may live the normal life, trying hard to conform, doing the right thing but underneath you know there is something missing, and the ego will use fear to ensure you stay normal and dissatisfied.

Not sure this is true? Sit on a bench in the middle of a city and watch the unhappy faces as they move in trance-like states through their lives – held in delusion by the collective and personal ego, iPods plugged in to drown out a reality they do not like and cannot accept.

Another method the ego uses is events. As an event happens, the ego will comment and tell you a story. "Dad spends more time with my sister. Therefore I am not as loved. There must be something wrong with me."

From this story, the ego will now search your life and events to find "proof" that this is true. It will select men for you who treat women as objects to be used, men who have no respect for the feminine. The ego will select these men and blind you to the mistakes that you are making. These men will prove to you, you are not loved.

It achieves this by making you listen to the story of you not being as loved as your sister and through that filter on your senses only allows in information that matches the belief. This filter works on your hearing, your sight and what you feel.

The truth is you are loved and equal in every way. If your father's ego did lavish more attention on your sister, that in no way diminishes you. As an immortal being, you can clearly have compassion for a man who is still in darkness and unaware of his actions and the results of them.

As an immortal soul, you know that this is of no consequence, and you become *awake* and are now attracted to a person who gives and shares love with you in the deepest and most intimate ways possible.

The third way the ego affects you is to filter everything that happens. It is always interpreting, always comparing, always altering. It is said that we never really experience reality. The ego ensures this is true. If you were hurt in your teenage years by a girlfriend, the ego now believes that all women equal pain. So to ensure its belief is reality, you could walk into a room with 49 loyal women and you would be attracted to the 50th who is disloyal. The others simply don't appear attractive to you. She will break your heart again. That is because the ego selected her.

The ego matches everything to its version of reality based on your past.

You cannot shut down the ego talking to you. Some may experience it as an incessant voice which never stops. Others will not notice it as much. They will tend to see themselves as nice people. Their ego is far more subtle.

However, if you become aware and raise your consciousness, you will hear the ego comment on everything. To escape its incessant influence, you cannot do it whilst still in the pond; you must move to the ocean. This involves a spontaneous experience or the practice of an experience through meditation. In these altered states you will have a greater connection to the divine and will raise your level of internal peace. The purpose of meditation is to pierce the veil that the ego places before your senses and experience what is real.

The Tao puts it succinctly:

Men possess It without knowing.

One then acts with virtue and honor which is inferior to Tao.
The less superior is to act with fear.
And the least superior is to act with disgrace.
This occurs because one does not have enough faith, and hence has no confidence.
The nature of Tao is distinguished by wordless teaching with the natural act of virtue without action.
As such, people would act effortlessly and harmonize with the Nature Tao.(4)

What Lao Tzu meant was you can use your morals and your beliefs as a guide but that is not *awakening*. Faith is based in experience of the divine, the nature of Tao. The divine is reached not by teaching but by being there and taking action effortlessly in harmony with the divine. To begin that process you must have right action combined with right thought.

Once you have connected with the divine, what bothered you before won't bother you now. As you loosen the bounds tying you to this false reality, you experience the peace that exists when you *awaken*.

The natural peace that is there for you at all times but you have forgotten what it is like.

Why do we have an ego?

The nature of the universe is a duality. The two more distinctive forces in the universe are the force of creation that builds and the force of destruction that tears down. As everything is energy in this universe and has vibration, so too, do these forces.

The Divine has a higher energy and higher frequency of perfection, total stillness, total love, which you cannot achieve in this universe. If you did you would cease to exist here. The ego has a lower energy that approaches total annihilation, or Death.

One is what you call the Divine, or God, and the other is the ego, or the Devil, Mara and many other such names. Therefore you are part of that duality. You have an area of your mind where you store all memories and record every single thing that you have seen, heard or experienced. In your normal everyday states you do not recall these things. They may be accessed in an altered state such as hypnosis or deep meditation or through a spontaneous spiritual event.

One portion of your mind stores all positive experience and is intrinsically positive. The other portion stores all negative experiences and is intrinsically negative. The ego of your mind does not share information or speak to the positive part. The ego has no access to the other information at all, including when decisions need to be made. When you do create access to the divine, it can provide you with a balanced view as it shows you reality.

Therefore, the ego can only use negative information in making decisions for you. These are sometimes called behavioural biases but are really the ego at work. It realizes, however, that you will not accept strategies that will obviously harm you. It thus offers strategies that seem to help you. Below are some examples.

"I am bored." The suggestion may be "Let's eat chocolate" – even though to alleviate the boredom you could exercise. Using its filter, your ego ignores the health cost.

If you were hurt by your relationships when you were small, the story you now listen to is "Relationships mean pain. Therefore let's avoid relationships." Or if you do have one, "Let's do things in it that push the other person away and prove my belief." This is despite your true desire to be loved.

"I want to have plenty of money to live well." The ego's solution will either be "Let's be tight with money and protect it", driving everyone around you crazy and making sure you don't enjoy it. Or alternatively, it will say, "I'm a really good saver and handle my money well, so let's enjoy it." You then wake up one day to find you have no savings as you spent all your money on toys and trinkets.

You may have been disappointed growing up. You or your family may have placed high expectations on you. Now your ego lives that every day. You are constantly judging yourself and others because your ego is the hardest on you. It never lets up. Even though good things may happen, it ensures you live in fear and anxiety that something bad is about to happen. You seem to attract these things. If only one small thing goes wrong, that is what your ego will have you focus on.

You learnt as a child how important it is to achieve. Now you have become so focused and driven by your ego that relationships suffer. Those around you never gain your full presence because your ego has you thinking of other things while you are with them.

Each of these strategies and the many others that the ego uses have the same common flaw. They are circular and return to the user, the result they are seeking to avoid.

You have an ego because it is an intrinsic part of the universe you occupy. Your way to peace is to recognize it and not to follow its insanity. The way to peace is the calm inside you that is your true nature.

Slowly you must know both your ego and your own true divine nature.

"Know Thyself," the oracle of Delphi said. This is the path to *awakening.*

How do we know what the truth is? How does the ego distort it?

The ego will adopt a belief in the divine if it keeps you deluded.

However, there is but one truth, you are the divine and the divine is you. Once you *awaken* you will no longer need this universe.

To quote *A Course in Miracles*:

> *Time and eternity are both in your mind, and will conflict until you perceive time solely as a means to regain eternity.*(6)

You cannot do this while you believe that anything happening to you is caused by factors outside yourself. You must learn that time is solely at your disposal, and that nothing in the world can take this understanding from you. The ego will use any belief system to hide that truth from you. Your ego is always seeking to place meaning on any event that happens to you in order to obscure the truth.

The ego will interpret the great holiday you won in a lottery as the universe rewarding you for being good. It can interpret the car crash you had as God punishing you. All these beliefs it creates are designed to have you attach to and believe in a reality you see with your eyes.

It will have you believe in science, it can make you believe in mathematics. It can have you believe in the power of positive thinking. It wants to have you believe in something that reaffirms the world around you and denies the reality you cannot see.

Hence *A Course in Miracles* says:

> *The distractions of the ego may seem to interfere with your learning, but the ego has no power to distract you unless you give it the power to do so. The ego's voice is an hallucination. You cannot expect it to say "I am not real." Yet you are not asked to dispel your hallucinations alone. You are merely asked to evaluate them in terms of their results to you. If you do not want them on the basis of loss of peace, they will be removed from your mind for you.*(6)

None of these beliefs the ego would have you adopt will lead you to the truth. This can only occur through your direct experience of the divine. No other person can give that experience to you, and only you can decide to claim it. It can never come from an ego-inspired thought system.

What is important to understand is that all thought systems are ego inspired. Every thought you have is ego inspired. This is how the ego keeps you attached to the false world in which you live. The second important point is not to adopt another belief system and deny the ego's existence. This is just creating an attachment to another belief system. The key is to *awaken* and then to walk the world experiencing only the divine within it.

The ego will also ensure you have a great desire for something. An addiction that keeps you attached to the ego. It could be sex, money, superiority, hard work, information, inferiority, chocolate, smoking, movies – anything that keeps you attached to something in this world that the collective ego has created.

Consider what the ego has you addicted to?

A Course in Miracles correctly says:

> *Every response you make to everything you perceive is up to you, because your mind determines your perception of it.*(6)

What do you mean by all thought originates in the ego? We have created many wonderful things with thought.

Yes, and the pride that you have in the power of your thoughts is justified. You created this universe by perceiving of it. That's how powerful you are. But your ego also created the delusion to keep you trapped here, suffering.

A Course in Miracles states:

The separation is a system of thought real enough in time, though not in eternity. All beliefs are real to the believer.(6)

The event of creation was jointly by you and the Divine. In that moment you had free will, but at the moment of creation the separation was felt and the ego was created by us collectively to comfort us. Like any living thing it wanted to exist, and it could only do that if its host did also.

All thought is of the ego because that is what it is. Thought.

Close your eyes for a moment. Wait. What happens? Thought arises, doesn't it – automatically. You do not want it to occur, so why does it?

If you do not have control over it, who does? Is it your thought, or does it arise when you have the intention of being quiet?

Thought can be used to understand the creation of the universe and to perceive the rules of how it operates, but only to a point. Past the point of creation thought has no use. It cannot explain what occurred because this is in terms of which thought has no knowledge.

To quote Stephen Hawking, "The beginning of real time would have been a singularity, at which the laws of physics would have broken down."(8) The ego can only explain what it has created, not what the divine has.

The ego does not understand peace because that is from the Divine. It seeks to upset peace because not doing so will allow you to remember.

You mention that the ego uses filtering. Can you explain what you mean?

There is no reality. Everything you see is processed through your senses. There is no color red. It only appears that way because of how our brains process the light reflecting off a surface. You describe those who see colors differently from most of you as color blind. Blind to what color?

The ego wants you to live in the past or the future. With filtering it uses the past. It can use an event in the past that created an emotional impact on you.

The movie, *Shallow Hal,* demonstrated this in a humorous way. Young Hal is at his father's deathbed. Unfortunately, his father, who was a preacher, is high on morphine. He gives Hal dubious words of advice about women, then passes away.

Now a young man, Hal seeks out women for pleasure and sees them as objects. The ego takes one event and makes a belief out of it, reinforcing it with pain. So every time Hal enters into a relationship, it ends. If he were to stay, the pain of loss would be too high for Hal to bear. As he mixes with friends who see women the same way, his behavior seems normal.

The ego uses this pain to energetically keep itself charged. It gives it fuel to keep going. Eventually love prevails in the movie and Hal falls for a woman who is unattractive and overweight but he loves her anyway because he can see who she really is on the inside. This is similar to *awakening*. He has come out of his ego-created delusion; the suffering and pain have stopped. He can see the truth and what matters. He is free.

Your ego takes any event and creates a belief from it. Those beliefs becomes global beliefs applicable to all similar situations. All men are ..., all women are ..., all bosses are ... You will therefore be sentenced to repeat the past.

There is one solution to filtering. Become aware. Raise your consciousness in order to see what the ego is doing. The moment irritation arises, pause, allow peace, or stillness, to arise. Seek your true nature and now observe the reaction. What is this really about? Do I have to react this way?

The true answer will be "No. This does not require me to respond this way." Master your awareness as a step to *awakening*.

How does the ego create separation?

The ego creates the arising of feelings by its definition of all things. It uses your senses to give a meaning to everything around you. This includes objects, things, events, all forms of form itself.

Only through these definitions can emotions arise.

It says "that" is good or bad as its two basic definitions. Nothing is intrinsically good or bad, only the ego makes such distinctions.

If it is good, then the ego will say you need it, even if it leads to what you do not want. If it is bad, it will reject it, even if it will give you want you want. Using the boredom example above, the ego offers you chocolate. It says boredom is bad, so you should have someone or something that is good. In this case, chocolate, even though, long term, chocolate is bad for you.

Emotions are caused by the polarity of form. It is either good or bad. One of those choices inspired by the ego's separation causes an emotion. Emotions cause desire, desire causes wanting, wanting causes action, action causes results, results cause karma. Karma is caused by the attraction of negative or positive energy/vibration to your consciousness.

Buddha spoke of this in the Pali Canon and Jesus did also when he said:

What comes out of a man is what makes him "unclean." For from within, out of men's hearts, come evil thoughts, sexual immorality, theft, murder, adultery, greed, malice, deceit, lewdness, envy, slander, arrogance and folly.(7)

He was referring to the creation of negative karma. This chain causes the negative karma which keeps you in illusion. Ceasing the cause of the emotions ceases the karmic effects and moves you closer to *awakening*.

Meditating without lowering the karmic effect is like weightlifting without the weights. Lots of puffing and no result. Many of you undertake the practices without having taken this step. Buddha was once asked a question about bathing in the Ganges River to purify himself. He responded by saying that the river was not going to purify him, only the eightfold path would do so.

Meditation is the same. It will not purify you. You can meditate eight hours a day, but without lowering your karmic footprint you will find it difficult to pierce the ego veil to clear sight.

The opposite of separation is love. Love is a natural result of *awakening*. It is the natural state of the divine.

Love in its purest form is not wanting at all. It is not giving either, it just is. You know if you are loved whether someone does for you or not.

The ego's form of love always involves a trade. You either do for the loved or they do for you. The divine's love wants nothing from you, it is always there. Hence we recognise it as the purest form of signpost of what we really are.

Love is about joining, not separation. Love brings together.

If I'm not my thoughts and feelings, who am I?

Everything you feel and think is subject to change and is constantly affected by what happens around you and how your senses and your ego interpret these changes. Your thoughts and feelings are based on an ever-changing self-image.

Inside you carry an imprint of how you should be and behave. That self-image is based in the ego. It is constantly updated depending on events that occur which cause you to make new decisions about the meaning of life and events.

You are not the same person you were five years ago. If you are what you think, feel and act like and that changes constantly over time, who are you really? The ego will attempt to give you the impression that "you" are a constant.

The ego is the master of many faces. You act like one person with a friend, like someone else at work and like another person with your family, someone different again when you are alone. The ego is master of many masks. There is no you, just a collection of behaviors that change and make up who your ego tells you are.

You change day by day and your ego's internal self-image guides how you react. The practices contained in Chapter 3 will guide you to alter this and be who you really are. If you follow the ego, it will create for you a spiritually aware mask that meditates and knows all the correct knowledge to espouse. It knows how to act as though it is aware.

The real you is part of the divine, it is truly *awakened*. It has no need to create a new image because it just is what it is.

How does the ego affect me at work?

In 360 Degree Reviews it is often found that leaders are unaware and reject feedback on their negative traits. These negatives are justified by leaders as an inherent part of their leadership style. (9)

Often leaders bypass the feedback, having no awareness of the effect of mood swings and outbursts, for example, on their fellow workers. These blind spots are the ego at work. This is the ego using another of its defenses, denial.

It is inherent in the ego to hide from you the effect on others of what you do or how you behave. That's how holocausts happen.

Have you ever found yourself being grumpy or just tired, and when your partner accuses you of that behavior, you respond with denial? That is an example of the central tenant of the ego's false construction of reality. It lets you use your senses to take in what matches its version of reality. The voice that says "Yes, I am a little grumpy right now and I need to take a break for a moment" is drowned out by the ego voice of denial: "What do you mean grumpy? I'm not grumpy. You're just picking on me as you always do."

Now the ego switches to its second line of defense, which is projection. "It's not me, it's them. I didn't give the orders to sack all those people, I'm just carrying them out." The ego operates just as easily at work as at home.

The ego can make you subtly resistant to being a team player. It wants you to stand out, to gain admiration. It can make you a passive resister at work saying yes but doing no. It can make you the star, always seeking glory above others. "I can make you try hard to have everyone like you," it says. It can make you intolerant of others' mistakes at work. It can make you want to do things your own way and ignore policy. It can make you miss things that were right in front of you that cost the company lots of money.

Not understanding or recognizing your ego will cost you a lot at work.

The practice of *awakening* draws your attention to when the ego is filtering reality. At work and at home.

I don't believe there is an ego. How can you prove it exists?

There are many examples of great thinkers and religious figures from the annals of human history who refer to the ego. Plato, Aristotle, Jesus, Buddha, Marcus Aurelius, Freud, to mention a few. It is however best to allow your own experience guide you on this question.

You will have experienced the competing voices in your head, which everyone has, one suggesting doing something and the other not. Which is you? Are both you? Now consider times when you have wanted something and the voice says "yes" and you know that this object of your desire is not what you really want or that it is not good for you. But you still get it anyway. An emotion rises in you and that emotion causes you to overrule your logical thought. Your logic does not win.

This is one of the primary mechanisms the ego uses to hold influence over you. It applies to anything you become addicted to – chocolate, alcohol, sex, relationships, fighting, drugs of any type.

That is the ego using the pain from past memories, both in this life and many others, to force you to react in a way you do not wish to. The ego tells you to use the addictive substance or behavior to relieve your pain and cover it over so you can deal with the world. The side-effects, however, are worse than the pain you must face and deal with. Feeling bored – take chocolate, feeling unsuccessful – take methamphetamines, feeling unloved – take drugs of any type. The source of these emotions is always the ego making you feel less, making you feel not enough, focusing on what you don't have, instead of what you do. That force, that compulsion, is the ego at work.

In some people that voice inspires depression by focusing on the lack in their life. It also creates anxiety by focusing on the future and what they may miss out on or will not have. Both these states are modern scourges of our culture and one of the principle reasons we take so many antidepressant and antianxiety drugs. These drugs don't solve anything, they cover up the underlying cause.

We all know there is no meaning to life.

The real cause of the ego's dominance is this lack of meaning in life, inspired by the ego who knows this to be true but must keep you occupied to ensure you have no awareness of it. If you did, then you would seek the truth. That's why the ego keeps giving meaning to everything and that's what keeps you lost and deluded.

A beautiful practice in awareness is to pause for a moment when an event that would normally upset you happens. Someone is mean to you, a lover leaves you, you don't get that pay rise, someone cuts you off in traffic. Normally the ego will rush to your aid. "I'll sort this out. Let me scream at them, let's burn their car, let's quit this job" it will say.

Now pause. Watch the ego, what it says, what it does. Become the observer of the ego. Separate it from you. Now you can know for yourself that it is separate to you. This is the ultimate proof that you can experience yourself.

Go even deeper into awareness. Consider thinking without the thinker, hearing without the hearer, seeing without the seer. We can be that clear if we choose to be. We can stand back from form and become the watcher of form rather than the reactor to form.

The greatest delusion the ego possesses is to have you believe those reactions are you. That you are the ego.

Once you truly experience this, the emperor wears no clothes.

Why do we need meaning?

Our ego needs both meaning and love, but it is a bottomless pit and can never be filled. The only true source of love is the divine and the portion of it that you possess in your soul, your consciousness.

The divine in you knows the truth and the real meaning of existence.

When you do not have the experience of who you are and you intellectualize the divine, you allow the ego to create meaning – even if you are agnostic and say there is no meaning. That is in itself a meaning. Therefore, the double bind now is you are on a large rock in the middle of a never-ending vacuum and sentenced to death, so when you die, it will have meant nothing.

To rationalize this, the ego will tell you that you should leave behind a legacy.

So in a vain attempt to mean something, you work to amass fortunes or academic achievements to carry on your name, or you hope to live on through your children, and ultimately you become caught up in the egoic belief that death is the end. Or you vainly focus on leading a good life and rely on values to guide you. Those values, though, lack emotion and attachment of the heart to the soul. They therefore become unfulfilling.

The ego knows you will not endure this very apparent flaw.

Owing to this intrinsic double bind, your ego latches on to something to give life meaning: children, devotion to a cause, a career, money, a religious belief. And at the end of your life, you look back and attribute some meaning to it.

The ego is always filtering, always giving meaning to everything around you. It makes everything mean something to you. A hand is not a hand, it is either attractive to you or not. A glass is not a glass, it's either the right shape or the wrong shape, you like what's in it or you don't. This becomes the principle cause of karma or non-escape from the ego. Every meaning causes a reaction to the meaning given by the ego, good or bad. This in itself is the form of attachment of which Buddha spoke. Meaning creates attachment. Once realized, this is profound wisdom.

The only true meaning is that you are immortal, you live on forever and you come back to this and many other lives as many times as is necessary to release yourself. The peace that comes from the truth of this experience and knowing this is indescribable. Viewed from this framework, you see the world as an observer, with everything experienced but no meaning given and no attachment generated, which brings you into alignment with divine peace.

Meaning either gives peace or it does not, and what you seek more than love is peace inside yourself. That peace eludes you because, until you come home to the truthful meaning of who you really are, it can never be found.

Many search all their lives for that peace. They travel the world helping many people, they seek it in looking pretty, in having many friends, in researching and understanding the universe, they go through many emotional partners to find it, they change jobs, countries, and it's still not there. You can only find it through experience inside yourself in altered deeper states. That is the only way to it.

It is a combination of the meaning being correct and allowing access to the experience of knowing the truth. Hence Jesus said:

> *Have you believed because you have seen me? Blessed are those who have not seen and yet have believed.(7)*

You must first prepare the ground with right action and right thought, then you can experience the truth.

Believing what is written, adopting a thought system, is merely a construct of understanding which will never achieve experience because all thought systems are based in the ego.

Experience is based in truth and personal realization.

I cannot tell the difference between my ego and myself.

Most can't, because they are using the very thing that the ego owns to understand something that it can never understand. You use mind to understand the ego. The soul is the home of what you really are, you must access your connection to the divine to experience the ego with clarity and awareness. This is the correct way to "see" the ego always wishes it to be reversed.

The ego will claim it understands the divine. It will build religions around it asserting understanding, whilst covering the real meaning in misinterpretation and misdescription because it does not understand what is really meant.

Many have written on and continue to quote the scriptures and other religious texts without experience of what is being spoken. They think they understand the words without having had the experience. There is no understanding, no realization of what is being conveyed, no experience. The ego has misled them.

Equally, the ego will lead many to claim wildly exotic experiences during meditation or religious ceremonies as what count. None of them do. They are just part of the experience leading to the truth, not the truth itself.

You must use your consciousness and focus to hold to what your task is.

The early gospels were mis-understood by ego and pulled apart and put back together in egoic ways that 50 to 100 years after Jesus's death could only reflect a lack of understanding of the actual experience he was trying to pass on. The same with Buddha's teachings. He said:

> *Don't blindly believe what I say. Don't believe me because others convince you of my words.*
> *Don't believe anything you see, read, or hear from others, whether of authority, religious teachers or texts.*
> *Don't rely on logic alone, nor speculation. Don't infer or be deceived by appearances.*
> *Do not give up your authority and follow blindly the will of others. This way will lead to only delusion.*
> *Find out for yourself what is truth, what is real. Discover that there are virtuous things and there are non-virtuous things. Once you have discovered for yourself give up the bad and embrace the good.*(1)

In your search to experience the difference between your truth and the ego's, you will be led off the path into the forest many times by the ego. Expect it. When you think you have it, the ego will fool you.

You will know when it is fooling you because there will be no peace in you; you will still feel unfulfilled.

Like Jesus's disciple, Peter, who failed many times, eventually you will know the truth.

In *awakening* there will be two experiences: your day-to-day life, earning an income, being a parent, finding a life partner, buying the groceries, posting on Facebook; and your spiritual search. The more you seek the truth, the more your life begins to fill with what seem like miracles – coincidences that should not be happening. The more peace you become, the more you attract.

What are the coincidences you refer to?

The positivity in this universe that is the divine always is sending you messages. They are there in that chance meeting with a person you haven't seen for a while who mentions a book you should read. You are passing by a bookstore the next day and you notice the same book. You buy it and, as you read, there is one paragraph that really sticks with you; there is recognition of something you needed to hear.

This can have a profound impact your life.

Lao Tzu says:

> *Mystic Te is profound and far-reaching.*

It can guide all things to return to their original nature.(4)

And Jesus said:

Watch therefore, for you don't know the day nor the hour in which the Son of Man is coming.(7)

He was referring to the signs that appear all the time but you miss because of distractions.

A Course in Miracles states:

You may insist that the Holy Spirit does not answer you, but it might be wiser to consider the kind of questioner you are.(6)

You have all experienced this; it happens all the time. But you become lost again and lose the connectedness of these events and what they really mean. You must be open to see these messages clearly.

Another way to pass through these doors to the truth is to take the time to be still and quiet. Coincidences will prompt you to be open to and begin the search for the truth, they will show you the way, but they are not the truth. The truth is an experience for yourself – one that you must have.

You must also allow yourself to believe and enter the place where you can have that experience, as this will confirm for you what the truth is.

How do I attract abundance?

The secret is to be in alignment with the divine, to remain connected to it during every day, even when not meditating.

Too many people seek to create from the ego: that merely results in a rollercoaster ride of have and have not. Things go well for a while and then they turn to disaster.

Being in alignment with the divine by *awakening* creates from the frequency of creation itself. The power of this is unlimited. That's why Jesus said:

> *Ask and it will be given to you; seek and you will find; knock and the door will be opened to you.*(7)

He was referring to the unlimited power of the divine.

The purpose of this power is to create. The purpose that the ego follows is to possess for itself. The more it accumulates, the more it can say, "Look at me, how great I am." In its limited understanding, it sees that it has one life to accumulate and it must rush to do so. It does not understand that what is needed is not things but the connection to what one really is.

When you have *awakened* and can remain in the divine, you will experience a natural accumulation of good karma. This attracts to you abundance.

The divine does not seek abundance for abundance's sake. It seeks it to be creative, but only from the truth. It does not seek abundance to be greedy or want more, only as a creative act that it then shares with others. There are many examples of this in the world today – many have achieved great wealth, yet given most of it away.

The result is the only thing that is important to the ego. The creation is what is important to the divine, as an extension of the path to *awakening*. If it assists the individual or many to *awaken*, then events will occur to assist you and others in this task.

The divines intervention is however limited by the act of its creation of us. Correspondingly we have full power of creation and what we have created cannot be over turned by the divine. It would not limit our power, so our collective ego must be seen for what it is. A mass delusion that will eventually be undone. The divine can however influence us to *awaken* through the veil the ego raises.

All creation is an act of drawing together again. Each act brings the divine closer to you and you to it.

As the ego seeks a result, once achieved it will seek another. It is always seeking more, no matter what has been achieved. If you can hear it rejecting what has been said in these pages as you read, it is because it must rely on itself to create and therefore to control as many things as possible to ensure a result. This may work for a while, but it accumulates negative karma as it moves away from the divine. Inevitably this causes events which are negative in nature to occur.

Seemingly the person whose ego is accumulating continues to grow in wealth, but not in abundance if you look carefully. Whilst they may be able to control this area of their life, in other areas they begin to suffer. This may occur in health or relationships which begin to break down. The negative karma eventually accumulates to the point where they suffer.

If they do not change and the wealth is passed on to the next generation, the negative karma continues to accumulate through the way in which the wealth is handled by the ego. The issue is not wealth but how it is handled.

There is a huge difference between wealth and abundance. The former is ego created, the latter from the divine. One lasts, the other does not. One involves becoming closer to the truth, the other further away from it.

The ego can create wealth but its form of creation is based solely on its need to be recognized, to be separate by being better than everyone else.

Experience and maintain the connection to the divine, and then create. It will last – not for the purpose the ego seeks but for the purpose of bringing all of us together. There can be no greater reason to seek the truth.

Why doesn't God just speak to us?

The divine speaks to you all the time. The way in this universe the divine speaks is through inner guidance, not through emotion but through a sensation of what you need to do. Some refer to these sensations as "gut feeling" or "inner knowing".

If you listen in the stillness, you will hear the divine. The divine also sends coincidences, or synchronicity, to reach you and point you in the right direction. In meditation, the small, still voice will speak and you will be clear it is not the ego and it is not you.

Lao Tzu explains it thus:

Hence, Tao gives life to all beings and Te nurtures, grows, fosters, develops, matures, supports, and protects them.
Tao gives birth to life and yet claims no possession.
It gives support without holding on to the merit.
It matures them but does not take control of.
This is called the Mystic Te.(4)

Tao is the divine and Te is the creative force. It does not interfere. It gives life and free will at the same moment. When you come to the truth is up to you. It is your choice.

The divine can also connect with you through altered states during meditation called trance states or when you have rare moments of connectedness that some call revelations or insights. These can only occur through preparation to purify your karma through right action and thought. Read Buddha's account of his enlightenment. He states the result of intense focus led him through the distractions that Mara put before him to finally seeing past lives, results of his karma and then enlightenment.

Buddha explained the real purpose to meditation, which is to go beyond what our normal senses show us to experience the truth and know in the experience it is real.

You must use intense focus to go beyond the white noise of the veil the ego raises to deny you peace. Prior preparation with correct action and thought will make this easier for you. Purifying what you put into your body also alters the vibration and "lightness" of the body.

The ego will throw up thoughts, fears and problems for you to think about. The practice must be to use your focus on the breath to remain steady and, suddenly, a calm place, a place of peace, will open for you. There will be a quiet mind and you will be guided on any subject you care to explore and you will know that voice is not yours and not the ego's. Buddhists call it luminescence.

Go deeper now into a direct experience of your life, your full and many lives. See for yourself why you are here. This is not imagination, this is as real as when you open your eyes. That is the message that thousands of prophets have sent to you. Know now that it is true. However be aware that this experience is merely pointing to the truth.

The divine can also influence you to connect with others. This occurs in moments when you meet and you know it's for a reason. The divine is the opposite of the ego. The ego is separation, the divine is connection. The divine is one, as you are all one.

Become awakened to these moments of divine intervention. If you follow them correctly without the ego claiming them as other proof that you are special and have been chosen, it will lead you closer to the divine.

This sounds like some New Age mumbo jumbo.

You live in a time when science now confirms what the ancient Indian Vedic texts said 4000 years ago. The world is energy. String theory confirms there are many universes coexisting in one. Time is relative, all moments are one. These are insights that came from clearly seeing reality 4000 years ago. Science can now do the mathematical calculations to prove it, but equally science has not come up with a unified theory of existence.

Logic does not have all the answers. Science cannot confirm what gravity is or how it operates, so knowledge does not explain everything.

Even Einstein said:

> *Science without religion is lame. Religion without science is blind.*(10)

For a man who peered beyond the veil of the obvious, he has words of experience and disbelief in the obvious that are worth heeding:

> *My religion consists of a humble admiration of the illimitable superior spirit who reveals himself in the slight details you are able to perceive with our frail and feeble mind.*(10)

Lao Tse said:

> *A wise man of Tao knows the subtle truth,*
> *And may not be learned.*
> *A learned person is knowledgeable but may not know the subtle truth of Tao.*(4)

Einstein again:

> *The true value of a human being is determined primarily by the measure and the sense in which he has attained liberation from the self.*(10)

The Buddha adds more to the truth:

Use your own feelings to determine what is true to you. What in your heart either resonates as truth to you or it does not.(1)

Buddha spoke of his many lives. Jesus did as well:

He answered and said unto him, Verily, verily, I say unto thee, Except a man be born again, he cannot see the kingdom of the divine.(7)

There are many examples of well-documented after-death experiences. If you consider yourself a person requiring proof, examine them for yourself on the website of the School of Medicine's Division of Perceptual Studies, University of Virginia.(11) However, nothing can substitute for your own direct experience.

To acknowledge your true form as consciousness is the first step in *awakening*.

Ultimately, only you can decide to take the journey and experience the truth for yourself. You cannot just read the words and say, "Yes, this is how it is." That is delusion, and most exist in that state. You must break free and find it yourself. A master cannot give it to you, they can only guide and point you in the right direction.

This knowledge has existed for thousands of years and is brought to you again in another form, *awakening*.

You mention stopping thought, isn't that meditation?

Yes, meditation is about ceasing thought; however, over the years we have lost what meditation is really about. When Buddha practiced it, he was still experiencing. In his story of finding enlightenment, he heard someone playing a sitar on the river near where he was meditating and realized that the string pulled too tight or too loose could not play the correct note.

There is an inner tuition that comes as knowing, in contrast to a thought that comes from the ego. That is the difference you must feel to experience and know the truth. Buddha used meditation as the door into alternative mind states, where he could access this intuition. He used his focus during meditation in experiencing the ultimate nature of reality. Once he saw and understood, he was enlightened, free from the constraints of the ego and knowing for himself the truth.

Meditation can be excellent for your health because it takes all stress away. This, however, is not meditation's true purpose. It's the ego that causes stress. When you meditate, its correct purpose is to enter an alternative state of consciousness, to pierce the veil of the ego, through which you can access your truth, the universal consciousness. It is not to sit there and Ohm your way to quietness. That is a fallacy. The Buddhists have a walking meditation where your eyes are open. You can practice as well by learning to access the Theta state to become awake and alert. You can also meditate to reach that state and see what truth is revealed to you.

Practice it, find the truth for yourself. That is how you should meditate. Meditation then becomes a practice to enter a state of knowledge. In it, you will have the experience of who and what you really are. You will know the difference between the divine's guidance and the ego's incessant voice.

Learn to use Rapid Induction Meditation to enhance and accelerate your journey and connectedness. There is information in Chapter 3 to assist you.

Seek experiences of past lives, but don't allow the ego to fool you with dreams. When really there, you will know the difference. Equally, do not seek these experiences for their own sake, so you can later speak of this life or that life.

Await with quiet patience and determination the lifting of the veil during meditation. Then you will know what these written words mean.

What is this base of belief you refer to?

The greatest cause of unhappiness, or suffering as Buddha called it, is the lack of meaning in life.

Intrinsically, life has no meaning of itself. There is no meaning to living on a rock, circling an atomic furnace, in the middle of a vacuum. The only meaning is the one you give it. Some people live to help others, some live to serve a religion, some live to eat, sleep and die, some live to hate and kill others. You all choose meaning and that determines what you then do. Everyone chooses a belief system for life, every single one of us. Even those who profess to be agnostics or skeptics still choose to believe they are agnostic.

This creates a frame of reference for everything they experience and see, including what you are reading now. They may look at the sunset and comment on how the sun rises because the planet revolves around it, but not feel the beauty and majesty of it. The frame creates what they can experience and can see. It either lets the beauty in or it does not.

The questions the ego never lets you ask are: How does this belief system serve me? Is it making me happy or is it making me sad? To be happy, to be at peace, to be free from the ego, the underlying belief system must provide a protection from delusion.

The ego always wants to trap you into serving money, sex, people, belief systems, work, anything that will keep you focused on this world and your body. It wants you to worship at the altar of an unreality that will never free you. The only escape is to see and experience the truth.

This does not mean that you cannot enjoy these things, but attachment to them, becoming lost in them and experiencing loss with them are what hold you to your ego as well. Again, please don't misunderstand my words. This does not mean you will not experience grief at the loss of a loved one or joy at the beauty of a sunset. You will. But there will also be a profound peace underlying that grief or joy because you know the truth.

What is this belief system, the only one that has ever been real. *A Course in Miracles*, the Bible, the Upanishads, the Koran all point to this truth, that you are immortal, you never die. You will be with your loved ones for eternity and you will keep returning until you have learnt and accepted who you really are. When we have all done this, there will be no further use for the universe. It will fade away, as science has also predicted.

Investigating past or future lives, in itself, is unhelpful. Experiencing them, as proof to yourself to change your point of reference, is helpful. It is one of the belief steps that is necessary to break free from the egoic mind that says it owns you and that is all there is to you.

Focus not on the past lives but the lessons enjoined to your karma from them. This is important as it unhinges the ego. The ego doesn't believe this at all, it only believes what it can see and touch. Nothing else is real. Its greatest fear is death. It believes that it will die and death will be its end.

You will not realize that this is what the ego makes you feel, even if you see yourself as a kind person who lives a good life. Underlying this is the belief that you will die. This you hate and fear because it makes no sense to you. Some hold the belief based in religion that they will live again, but this is really just a hope. "This is what I should believe," the ego says. Becoming one with the divine is not truly known; it is a mental construct that the ego has built, so you feel temporarily safe, but it's not known through experience.

Once you *awaken*, you will accept the truth, the reality of what and who you are, and then you will have peace – real peace.

Without the experience of this being true, you can never become enlightened and you can never really have peace. The day-to-day experience will be of dissatisfaction. An underlying unhappiness that you never speak of with anyone, but which sits inside you like a stone.

This immortality sounds like a dream, too good to be true, so what is enlightenment?

To be free from the ego and continuously connected to the divine, that is enlightenment. It is to *awaken*.

Awakening is there awaiting you, even if you are seeking it somewhere else. It is immovable.

It is not some place to be reached. That is the ego distorting the truth and making it into another "thing" you must have. The truth is something you already possess as an experience inside you. That is what you must reach.

Buddha called it freedom from Mara; Jesus knew it as freedom from the devil whom he confronted when he went into the desert. You must all go through this, in this life or the next 100, but at some point you will want to face it. This could be your time and you will know if it is. That is why you are here now reading these words.

I have had many conversations with people searching for something. That something is not in India or Nepal or in a book. You can find enlightenment washing the dishes, you can find it by being aware and present to what is happening, in your awareness of what the ego is saying to you.

The search for enlightenment in itself can be a trap. If you say to yourself during meditation that you haven't reached it yet or that it's frustrating to listen to your ego all the time, that is the ego speaking.

Buddha reached his enlightenment by retreating into the forest after realizing that asceticism was not the answer; the middle way was. Then, in one night, whilst deep in altered states from meditation, he was tempted by Mara (the Sanskrit word for the ego). He was offered women, riches, kingdoms to divert him from the truth.

Jesus went into the desert for "40 days" and was tempted by the devil (another word for the ego) promising great kingdoms and riches if he would only follow what the devil said. Both stories are the same, and both men forced their egos to collapse through the power of their concentration in order to experience the truth.

All journeys to the truth face the same challenge. Your ego will do anything it can to preserve its own existence. Everything is energy and the ego is energy, a vibration of thought and frequency that you can tap into or out of. If you raise your own energy above that of the ego by changing your brain wave pattern, you will "escape" the ego.

Enlightenment is to realize the ultimate reality of nature and why you are here, not some theory but your own personal experience in attaining a state of such pure connection to the divine that the truth is revealed. Buddha made a decision after his enlightenment not to attempt to teach others what he experienced because he felt they would not believe him nor would it assist them to become enlightened. He developed, instead, a system to assist others to achieve enlightenment for themselves.

Some of what you read here may shatter your carefully constructed ideas of reality. That is a good thing, as those ideas hold you to a distortion of the truth.

There are many ways to experience the truth. Ancient tribes would chant as a way of altering their level of consciousness.

Think about a word.

What is it? It is merely your vocal cords sending out a vibration, an energy that your ear then interprets to mean something. Any emotion has a vibration to it. Anger can be felt as vibration when you are in a rage. If another is shouting, it can also be felt by you. Equally, love is a vibration that can be felt when directed or sent to another. It can be felt in a group of people in a room as a palpable force. That force can be tapped into and used by you to take your vibration to a higher level, one that is focused on helping others.

The ego also has a vibration. You can walk into a gang nightclub and feel the negative vibration. So the ego is a palpable force that surrounds you, and you can choose to connect to it by listening to it and lowering the vibration of your thoughts, or you can raise them up by directing your focus and thoughts to a higher vibration to escape it. Meditation allows you to do this by altering your brain waves.

On his dying bed, the Buddha has been quoted as saying to Ananda, his personal servant:

> Be lamps unto yourselves. Be refuges to yourselves. Take yourselves to no external refuge. Look not for refuge in anyone beside yourselves. And, those Ananda, who either now or after I am dead, shall be a lamp unto themselves, shall betake themselves to no refuge, but holding fast to the truth as their lamp, holding fast to the truth as their refuge, shall not look for refuge to anyone beside themselves, it is they who shall reach to the very topmost height.(1)

What is enlightenment not?

It is not adopting belief in reincarnation, that everything has a purpose, that we are all divinely guided and numerous other belief systems about the divine.

While these point in the right direction, they in themselves will not bring an *awakening*. The ego can easily use them to keep you in delusion. Simply believing that everything will be okay does not end suffering. You can still suffer. The ego will take this and use it to keep you focused solely on the mantra: all is good. Thus your business fails, your marriage falls apart and numerous other important things in your life are not attended to. That is not enlightenment, that is not higher awareness. That is delusion.

The ego would love you to adopt strict religious views, thinking that those who do not follow them are fallen or damned and claiming that yours is the one true religion and that other religions have no right to exist. You will know when someone's ego is speaking to you. It will be adamant that it is right, that its views are those that must be followed. That fanaticism is evident throughout the world in the force of terrorism. Any form of extreme belief is ego inspired. It will not allow other points of view to be considered. It does not want you to *awaken*.

This also applies to spiritual beliefs. When you think you are there, that is when you are not. When you are striving for something, that is the ego. When you hide behind a wall of "it's all okay," that is also the ego.

Many religious practices and beliefs have been distorted by the ego and, rather than provide freedom, actually keep you in delusion. While close to the original meaning, over time these practices have been distorted and the truth has been lost. For example, the current version of prayer is not direct communion with the divine but your ego pleading for something that it needs or wants. Genuine prayer is to reach for and receive clarity from the divine, rather than the other way round where your ego seeks to gain something for itself.

These practices were developed early by the Christian church as a means of instilling power in the church and the priests as the sole conduit to the divine, where all prayer and faith must be placed if you were to reach the divine, instead of teaching the truth as spoken by Jesus that only through the divine in yourself can you reach the divine. This is why Buddha adopted the middle way, realizing there was a place for all views but gently guiding people to the truth, their ignorance being not from malice but from a lack of knowing.

Whilst many beliefs are in alignment with the truth, only in direct experience can you truly know the divine. Then and only then will you know what the truth is.

What good does finding enlightenment really do for me? Why do I need it?

There are two types of people living today: those who are aware of their pain and those who ignore it. Both are influenced by the ego.

If you know you are in pain because of past events that have occurred to you, you know that your ego has you living in the past. The ego is always reaching into the past and placing the memories right in front of you. An event in the present will trigger pain from those past events and you will react in the same way as before. You may have been hurt by a past relationship, so now you avoid them to avoid the pain. When you were little, children were mean to you, so now you act as though you are shy. You were abused and now you relive that abuse every day.

Some egos make themselves feel okay by being superior to others either intellectually, or through their possessions, fame or title. What all people caught in their ego's delusion experience, is a lack, a searching for something that is not present in their superiority. Some choose suicide to escape this feeling of lack. Some very famous people demonstrate this principle at work.

Others may live normal middle-class lives, where they want no disruption, where they ignore the sadness in their spouses' and children's eyes, which is there because they are not really present, or may be there but their heart is not open and they are not really receiving the others' love. While they may profess to love their spouse and children, that is very different to being joyous and expressing their love to them.

Many people pretend that all is okay by wearing a facade of happiness, underneath which they are miserable because life has no meaning amidst the endless parade of faces and events. If this is you, this is merely another form of ego influence. The ego will feed on your sadness and continue to generate and select events to create more of the same for you. The ego prefers you to be in the pain that you know than either one you don't or one that could bring joy. The ego can ignore current pain and pretend all is okay.

Many couples are locked into relationships that are controlled by their ego. The ego has led them to live in the same house but never really connect with one another. They may be together for a long time, but they have settled into a form of ego relationship where it is safer to stay together rather than leave. The ego has deprived them of the true feeling of love.

The ego drives many to seek fulfilment through their children or through acquiring things, through sickness to gain attention, through drugs to end the pain of some tragic emotional event, through fighting with their spouse to generate excitement. The ego's ways are many but all will create pain and drive you to not be who you really are.

To be without the ego is to seek happiness in your truth and joy in the place that is truly home.

Please explain what to *awaken* means?

To *awaken* is to have a direct personal experience of the divine through an altered state and maintain that connection all the time. Once you have completed the lessons and taken your ultimate journey, you now focus on others joining you.

You no longer have the filter of the ego between you and life. You know your soul is part of the divine and is immortal. That knowledge transforms your reactions because in truth nothing can hurt you, fear is gone. Inside, there is a permanent stillness that is the mirror of what the divine is – it never leaves and pervades all you do.

You are calmer and clearer than before. Life is now a journey that is taken at a leisurely pace. There is no need for thrill seeking because life is the biggest thrill of all now you can see the grand panorama of it all.

The inner sense of peace and contentment is palpable and will not leave you. You know that what you see is false, "a prison for the mind", to quote *The Matrix*.(12) Now free of delusion, negative emotions are not felt in the same way. You know they are there because you are human, but you do not choose to follow them. That does not mean you feel no emotion. Quite the contrary! You will experience joy at seeing a flower opening or the beauty of a child's face, for in truth they will be enhanced.

The ego casts a veil over everything. It's like watching life through a fog. Once you *awaken*, the fog lifts. The colors are brighter, the experiences deeper. The ego filters everything. The flower looks beautiful till you wonder when it will rain, or did you pay the credit card statement? It always interferes with your experience of the now, as Eckhart Tolle explains in his book, *The Power of Now*.(13)

After *awakening*, you are not pulled into the future to worry about what may or may not occur because you know that you are safe with whatever occurs. You know whatever the event, it will be in accordance with the divine and you trust the outcome. Not because of a belief, but through truly knowing. This accumulates positive karma.

Equally, you are not attracted to the past where old patterns keep occurring to ensure you get results that are the same as in the past. The ego can only connect with you in the past or in the future. It cannot rest in the present. While meditating, notice that when you are distracted the thoughts which keep occurring always involve the future or the past, never the present.

When you are *awakened*, only the present arises for you. There can be no other time that you will experience because, in reality, there is no other time.

Even if you have problems to deal with, there is a calmness that pervades you moment to moment. There is no projection to the future as to what might occur. You deal with life in the moment rather than based on what happened in the past or what could occur in the future. You are aware of the possibilities of what may happen in the future, but you are not attached to those possibilities. You trust more. You have an inherent sense that it will all work out for the best.

You do not hear the ego's voice. It ceases and gives up, as it slowly dies and moves to its next host to torment. Suffering, as Buddha stated, has ceased.

Decisions are clear. There is no conflict internally between two voices with different opinions. You are certain what road you should take because you naturally rest in the divine. Every decision is literally guided by the divine.

You can see how everything is interconnected, how every moment is meant for a purpose. Every encounter is significant as each person moves along their life journey. You understand how we are all connected and you experience a sense of wonder at the beauty of the truth's grand design.

All is designed to bring you home.

How do I do this? How long will it take?

First you must decide this journey is important to you, that you wish to focus on the ultimate journey and make it central to your life.

Then there are the levels of the journey. First, there is removal of the patterns of behavior you have learnt in this life. These must be removed so that you have a clearer view of reality. Without their removal, reality is distorted and will always be a reflection and repeat of the past, or a false impression of the future painted by your ego.

There are many ways and practices to achieve this. The path is your choice. This is an important step because it brings self-awareness, the ability to become aware of the watcher who sees what you are doing. This is the presence of the divine in you.

Most people have no self-awareness. They instinctively react to what happens to them with little or no conscious thought. Someone is rude to them, and road rage takes hold. They will say later it was the rage that took hold and not really them. Others may have been hurt because their mother died when they were young and their father abandoned them. Such people now go from relationship to relationship, wanting the relationship, but never really committing. Yet others may have shut down because the love that was given to them when they were young had conditions and they now view love as a commodity to be bought and sold and never really given or received without conditions.

The way of the ego is as varied as the sunset. Becoming aware of these patterns of unconscious thought is the beginning of awareness and freedom.

Once this has been achieved, you can focus on living in accordance with the truth of who you are, the values of your heart – honesty, living and showing love, and making right choices, in accordance with the values of your soul. These values are universal. They build karma. They build it because they are moving in accord with the divine in order to connect with it. As karma builds, so does awareness and consciousness and at some point you will become clear about the unreality of the world around you.

Many at this point fall into a trap. They begin to listen to the ego, which can use this quest to *awaken* as another form of attachment to this world. The key here is to be patient, not to force *awakening*. If you feel a need for a result, that is the ego speaking. This must be a period of grace.

At some point you will experience grace and you will see, hear and experience the world differently. Even the Vedic texts from 4000 years ago spoke of the moment of grace from Krishna (another word for the divine).

Now, what used to make you react no longer does. Worries are no longer worries but expected changes in your path. You become present and accepting of what is. You accept that which occurs without ego-inspired thoughts that it should be another way.

Don't focus on the negative that can now be seen. You will see pain in the vast majority of people's eyes. You will feel sadness about what the ego is doing to our planet. What you must focus on at this point is the beauty of the world and pouring your love into it as much as possible, even if in the beginning of this stage just to those who are close to you, your family and friends.

Don't be fooled by the ego and do this from a sense of "this is what I should be doing now". Being pious is not the truth.

Don't ask when this will occur or how you will recognize when you have gone past this point into grace. You will know when it arrives. You will be as clear about it as staring into the sun. A sense of peace will be in you that no event in your life can shift – not loss, not an argument, not death. At this point you will trust that everything is happening as it should. You now are patient and awaiting what the world will bring to you.

Beyond this is the final step, one that allows you to experience full faith in the divine, the creator of everything, not the religious God but the one that you sense is here. The faith is not forced because you know with certainty and through experience that events and people occur for you on a path that is clear. There is no doubt; the belief is based not on dogma but experience of the divine.

Now you know you have arrived, but even in having arrived there is no sense of success or achievement. It was inevitable. Nothing has changed – you still wash the dishes and take out the rubbish – but there is an underlying joy in the experience of being immortal.

How long it takes is not up to your ego, which always wants things now and is driven to achieve them in a rush before it dies. When you know you are immortal, there is no sense of rushing, just inevitability. Few of you really believe this statement because few of you have reached this point.

This is also not a place devoid of emotion. Rather the reverse. Joy, peace, fulfilment are plentiful because that is who you really are. Fear, concern, worry, self-doubt are all absent as these belong to the ego.

If this is what we are meant to have, why is it so difficult to achieve for most people. Why doesn't God just give it to us?

You are here to have an impact on the universe. You are here to raise the vibration of the universe to a higher level. It is not a matter of the divine withholding anything from you. You are the same energy as the divine. Hence, when he said, "I and the father are one", Jesus was referring to the energy, the soul of who you are, as being the same as the divine.

You are here because you chose to be here, but when you came you forgot this as you connected to the ego. It is only in the light of an altered state of consciousness that you can remember. It's only when you withdraw your senses from the influence of the ego, or Mara, that you can again "see". Hence the words, "I was blind but now I see."

In this higher state you can access the insights that are available to us all. Most of you will not slow down and be in silence long enough to allow this to occur. Meditation is one road to allowing the connection to the divine to occur. Kinesiology and dream-like states as you awake, sit quietly and allow grace to occur are others.

There are stages to higher states and by gradually withdrawing your consciousness you must go through those states. That does not mean you will not exist or be or function in the world. It is not necessary to withdraw and take on the life of a monk in a cave to achieve this. That is one path, but not a necessary one.

Allowing your self to be conscious that this is what you want and allowing time to reach these states are critical prerequisites to beginning the journey.

Why are the messages and signs from the divine so subtle?

There are two opposite forces in the universe. One is the divine sending you a call to *awaken*. The other is the ego which is seeking to mask it. It does this by delusion, which encourages you to miss the messages when they are right in front of you.

It hides the call by making every event seem normal and lost in the random happenings of the day.

All events have meaning. It is in how you view the event that it will be seen by you as either a message or a random event. The ego will always see it as a random event. The more you connect with the divine, the more you will see it as a sign.

It's not that the signs are subtle, it's that the ego is always seeking to hide the message so you do not receive it.

Why are the results of not listening to the signs so severe?

They appear severe because, in missing the sign or message, you become more aligned to the ego and follow its strategy, which often results in disaster.

Why does God allow bad things to happen?

When you have reached higher stages of awareness that is not a question you will ask.

It will be clear to you that there are no bad or good things; it is the ego that makes such separation. Nothing is intrinsically good or bad. It is the ego always seeking to make you separate that creates these distinctions.

Is killing bad? Many would say yes. Then why is killing during war called something else?

It is intent that makes an act right or wrong. Right being closer to the divine. Wrong moving further away.

You attribute bad things to the divine's intent to do bad. That is not in the nature of who you are. Therefore, it is not in the nature of the divine. The truth is: the divine's nature and yours is one and the same, they cannot be distinguished.

Your true nature has no intent to do bad, only to become one again with the divine and bring all to the same place. The ego uses that intent for one reason, to cloak it in the same cloth as anything else the ego does: to separate.

People will do bad things because they believe the ego's view of the world. A world without the divine appears to be a lonely, cold universe with no meaning. Therefore, it is easy to believe in some other form of belief or extremism. Hence, terrorism is ego based and a distortion of the true desire to connect rather than separate. For the follower of the ego, this will accumulate negative karma.

The negative action attracts more negative energy, or vibration, which in turn creates more negative action upon the soul of the participant. "Bad things" happen because of the ebb and flow of negative karma. Once the bad thing has occurred, the karma is paid. It neutralizes the energy and the energy is equalized again.

If you continue to do bad things once the event occurs, then negative karma builds and you attract more bad things. However, every event is a chance to begin again. That beginning occurs with every event, including a birth. It is another opportunity to fulfil your ultimate purpose. Now there is a chance for awareness to rise again. All roads lead to one inevitable place: the divine.

This question arises because, if the ego can convince you that the divine is inherently evil, then you will remain in delusion.

Can the ego be used for good?

It is helpful to focus on the positive in life. However, this belief system will not assist you to *awaken*. You may be the most positive person, repeating daily mantras and seeking guidance from angel cards. This is not *awakening*. It is moving towards it, but it is not the practice that will achieve it.

Many become lost in practices that bring temporary relief. They are like bandages on a wound: until the correct salve is applied, the wound keeps festering, requires redressing and does not heal.

Your question comes from the desire to focus on the positive rather than the negative. The ego can use positive emotions as easily it can negative emotions such as depression or anxiety. It can make you so positive that you refuse to see the negativity you wreak on others. It can also be so positive that you do not wish to see your ego and what you do to yourself and others by following it.

The ego is not designed to do good or bad; it is designed to keep you in delusion. This, of itself, is neither good nor bad as these are relative terms applied to this universe – to yin and yang. However, the ego is a hindrance in that it slows down your use of time to achieve your ultimate journey, to reach the divine.

The ego cannot be used to *awaken*. Any attempt to use the ego in others is your ego at work. If you wish to help others, you can call to the divine in them to *awaken*, then wait patiently for them to respond.

Isn't this just a rehash of what others have said? There's nothing new here.

The truth has been presented many times. More than can be counted. It will be presented many more times. This is but one. Some will hear and see, some will not. That will be determined by their own desire to be free.

The truth needs to be presented in many ways as the ego is always seeking to delude, to cover up and distort what is real. Sometimes it takes but one word in one book for someone who is ready to begin to see. Others are in the early stages of *awakening* and will respond to messages in another medium. If this message is for you, you will know. If it is not, I pray that another message will reach you. It may be a song, a book or an advertisement on TV.

The ego will attempt to categorize the truth as Hindu or Sufi or Christian. It is, however, none of these.

Only the ego will want to put a label on the truth, attempting once again to lose the power of the truth by categorizing it as something other than what it is. "Ah," it will say, "that's the same as Buckminster Fuller said." Or "That's what St Augustine said." The words are not the truth. They merely point to it. It is not intellectual understanding; it must come from direct experience for you personally. It cannot be done any other way.

Other sources are quoted here to show that the message of the truth has been presented many times in many ways, but they all point to the same place.

Be assured that the message is all around you every day. In events, conversations, coincidences. Many are not searching for it, so it is missed. There are many, many opportunities for you to *awaken* and experience life as you were meant to.

This is merely another. Please accept it and allow it to speak to your heart and your soul.

What is karma?

Karma is a Buddhist and Hindu belief: what you put in, you get back.

The same principle applies in physics: for every action, there is an equal and opposite reaction. You can see this operate in your current life. Be cruel to someone and there is a consequence; give love and there is a definite return.

The ego, however, will have you expect that when you give, you should always get something in return. The ego is always judging, always comparing each measure of what you give with what is given in return, and it always finds it lacking because the ego is a bottomless pit. As it is separate from the divine, it always senses that it lacks something but cannot understand what it lacks. It must deny the existence of the divine for itself to exist.

Equally, over your many lifetimes you build up a vibration or energy of karma that you bring to each life. Look at any baby. It is evident that they are shaped by the experiences that they have in their life. It is also equally evident that they come with a personality that contains their karma, the imprint of who they are, how they react to life and what they expect from it.

Some babies are very quiet and placid and sleep well. Others are full of energy and animated, always seeking experiences that lead them into trouble.

Many ask: "How can you be good all the time?" Under the influence of your ego, you can't; it will be forced. It will be a belief that you should be good. If you are doing good to attract good karma, that is the ego speaking. In the divine, you will naturally do good because that is who you are.

When you have *awakened*, the connection to the ego is lost and the ongoing negative karma is no more. When you follow the ego into an incorrect action, a negative vibration occurs, which attracts more negative karma. Karma can be thought of as the vibrations you accumulate.

When you have found the truth, karma is balanced because the energy, the vibration you now exist in, is love and peace.

Even if you have spent your life devoted to helping others, for your karma to be balanced you must experience the truth, as awakening must precede the action of giving, not the other way round, as many religions would have you believe. It's the divine connection that allows karma, the negative vibration, to dissipate. Delusion cannot stand before the truth.

Does this mean you will be perfect then? No, Jesus lost his temper in the temple. Buddha walked away from his community when they were fighting. You exist in this reality and the ego will still influence you. However, the peace never leaves you, the love is always there and you are not deluded by the ego.

In your journey through many lives you will switch between masculine and feminine bodies, depending which will serve you best to *awaken*. Your karma has an influence on this. Karma attracts the parents and life you are born into – each one a new opportunity to *awaken,* each circumstance reflective of your accumulated karma.

As you *awaken,* your karma changes. Death is nothing anymore; it is merely a transition to another reality, a door to another quality of life that is always immortal.

If I'm reborn many times, are you saying nothing matters, that I can do whatever I like?

Many people do exactly that, but if you observe their lives there are consequences. Saddam Hussein, Gaddafi, Hitler – all met fates that reflected the way they lived their lives. Karma is an effective means of drawing us back to the divine.

It is evident that you can do whatever you wish, but most of you are held back by culture and other beliefs from doing so. Nothing really stops you from doing what you decide except for your beliefs. However, in doing what you decide, karma will be evident in the effects and consequences. It is merely a device to bring you home.

If you do incorrect things, then you will move away from the divine, for that is not its nature. If you do good things, you will move closer to the divine. There is no judgment in these statements, just observation as to how reality is constructed.

There are also practical consequences of doing whatever you wish. Commit murder and you will likely spend time in jail, cheat on your wife or husband and a divorce will likely follow, spend unwisely and bankruptcy will be the result. These results are not certain; however, karma is certain – it operates clearly and efficiently to provide guidance to draw you back home.

The result is inevitable, as *A Course in Miracles* states:

> *It is a required course. Only the time you take it is voluntary. Free will does not mean that you can establish the curriculum.*(6)

The time it takes is up to us. The reality, of course, is that time does not exist and the union with the divine has already taken place. It is only in this universe that it appears not to have yet occurred.

What about the Bible and God? Where do these fit in? Don't you believe in God?

The Bible was written by men and is a combination of the old Judaic beliefs and the refined message that Jesus brought. He did not write it down; it was written many years after his death by people who had not met him. Other writings were discarded by the church authorities because these did not suit what they understood the message to be.

Over time, the ego became involved in the interpretation of the writings. "An eye for an eye" refers to karma, but the ego has twisted this to mean revenge. "No one comes to the Father except through me" interpreted correctly means grace and your consciousness, which is spoken about in this book.

If you refer to the divine as a being who sits in judgment of you and your actions, there is no belief or basis for this in any spiritual writings – only misinterpretation over centuries by men lost in their egos, who used religion and the divine as indoctrination to control others. That legacy is present in various writings, and is no different from what Hitler or other dictators, lost in the ego, have done more recently to control others.

God, as you may refer to it, is the force behind the universe. It is also the Tao, the omega, whatever term you wish to apply. It seeks to bring the universe together, to balance the forces – to bring the creative forces and destructive forces into one again. Your part is to be the generator of positive karma until you have brought yourself and many others home. When the Divine is used for love, it can be useful to bring you to your heart, your own essence, which is also divine. That is why the Buddha said:

My heart, thus knowing, thus seeing, was released ...(1)

A belief system of any sort will not bring what you seek. It will not bring actual experience.

The Divine is beyond religions, which are thought systems to explain something that can only be understood in direct experience.

Only your own searching on the right path will allow you to experience the divine.

Who are you to be teaching this?

Many have delivered this message over thousands of years and many will continue to do so in the future.

Why me? It is my time and my karma to have had this experience and so I am able bring the truth to you. It will happen to you once you have reached a point where you are tired of living controlled by the ego.

Maybe it is your time now? For many people it may take many lives until it is theirs. That is the beauty of the divine: it is very patient.

What is the soul?

It is the spark of the divine in you as in all of nature. You can feel the life – the creative force – in a tree or standing watching the ocean or the night sky. It is in everything.

That's why Jesus said:

> Cleave a [piece of] wood; I am there. Raise up a stone, and you will find me there.(7)

In you it is your consciousness. Emotion is felt through the heart and not the head. With the correct guidance, your heart can become your door to the divine. You are unique amongst all sentient beings in your ability to use your heart in this way.

The Tao said:

> Can one unite the body and the spirit as one and embrace the Oneness without departing from the great Tao?
> Can one achieve harmony with such gentleness by holding on to the true spirit within as if the innocence of an infant?
> Can one free oneself from worldly knowledge and cleanse one's mind, so that no faults shall be made?
> Can a ruler love his people by governing with the natural Way without personal intention?
> Can the mystic gate to all life essence be opened or closed without the virtue of the mysterious nature?
> Can one gain the insight of nature and become a wise person without the effort of action?(4)

Lao Tzu was not asking questions. He was posing these as Zen koans, or parables. A question answering itself. The answer to each is yes.

Your consciousness can be felt through your heart. It can never be felt in the mind, just imagined as a concept. That's why many intellects caught in the ego deny its existence. Feeling it is an experience and the experience confirms the existence of your consciousness, but only once your pain has been removed, once the patterns have ceased. The heart is not accessible when all feeling is numbed.

A mechanism of the ego to ensure you experience no pain is to teach you to become emotionally numb. Many children learn how to do this and, being unaware, they follow the ego's instructions to create a block to emotions. They can literally know what they should be feeling, but they do not experience any emotions in their body and their heart is subsequently shut off from compassion and empathy.

Children who self harm can achieve this with their body as well. Self-harming makes them feel again. Unfortunately, they have numbed their emotions and to feel anything they need to cut. They acknowledge that there is a flood of relief when they do. The way out from this delusion is to allow themselves to open their hearts again.

However, the ego says, "Don't do that, you will be hurt again like before. Numbness is the road to safety." The ego prefers the harsh physical pain to the emotional pain it seeks to avoid. The ego of course has no knowledge of the heart or its connection to the divine. Its strategy is to close off and shut down.

This behavior is an indicator of a larger and prevalent problem. A large number of the world's young people are desperately seeking meaning that only connection with their consciousness can give them. They feel lost and want to find real purpose and meaning beyond the mundane life they feel awaits them. If you have a child like this, or know of one, speak with them about their consciousness and its connection to the divine. It is the way out for them and it is your responsibility to show them this way.

Awareness of the soul only confirms the existence of the truth. It is not the truth, nor the experience of it. Nor can the divine be accessed through it. It is, like many things, merely a pointer to the truth and your own experience of the divine.

Chapter 2

PRACTICAL AWAKENING

Why do some people seem to go through abusive relationships and then be attracted to the same type of person again?

Your karma, both good and bad, is created in interaction with others until you have balanced the energy, both positive and negative, it offers. It can be a source of suffering or *awakening*.

The ego always stays with what it knows. At a personal level, it learns from your personal life history. If you come from an abusive family, it will be attracted to what it knows. It will value abuse above trying something new. Your ego may decide early in your life that you are not worth much and based on that filter on the world it will seek out someone to treat you accordingly.

This principle is used by the ego in all patterning. Once it learns how to do something, it will stick with it even if it brings you pain. A central tenant of the ego's belief system is: "Better the pain I know than the one I don't."

So it is not difficult to understand why one would return to the inflictor of pain many times until awareness arises to end the cycle. Sometimes that does not happen in this lifetime and great pain and sadness are experienced.

This is not necessary for learning. If you have enough awareness to see what the pattern is, then you can release from it.

Take a moment and be still. Allow the ego to arise within you. You know its feeling. You have felt it before. You will feel the emotion that it brings from the past into the present within you now. Just watch it, become aware of it. Now you can see that you are the observer of the ego and not one with it. Now you are your true self.

This is the practice of awareness. When an event occurs, you can stand by and watch your own reactions – amused at the crazy thoughts, feelings and reactions that the ego delivers to you but not accepting any of them.

What occurred in the past does not live in the present. It can only be here now if you allow the ego to bring it.

Awareness dispels the ego from taking hold. It is a powerful practice.

What about my relationship with my spouse, how does the ego operate here?

The ego loves this special relationship above all others but not in the way you may think. It loves it because within a special relationship it can use love for its own purposes.

The ego is always concerned with one person, itself. Within a relationship it will always be focused on how it can satisfy its needs. If it has to give to get, it will do so as long it receives in return. If it doesn't, then manipulation, either subtle or direct, will follow.

Subtle manipulation will cause a wall of separation to be felt. Emotions are felt as well as displayed and a partner can sense when the other is closed. The ego will project that separation on to the partner who will hold back a little in the relationship, ensuring the partner will respond in the same way. This completes the ego belief that love is not real. It believes companionship and safety is sufficient.

Direct manipulation is reserved for escaping – escaping by not being present and finding satisfaction with another while keeping the safety of the current partner intact. If the current lover finds out, then that can be leverage to convince them to change their ways. If not, then a move to the new lover is assured. Fighting and drama will follow, adding to the story the ego will build to finally convince them to leave guilt free.

Your personal ego learns about relationships by watching and modeling your parents as you grow. It takes on the worst of the patterns, both spoken and unspoken. If two parents never argue, it can reach the conclusion that you don't argue in a special relationship. With a lover, it will attempt to keep the peace, resulting in a huge wall of anger and resentment because nothing real is ever discussed.

The ego can convince by telling you that your lover doesn't love you and that the best way to deal with them is to give in all the time. Your lover's ego quickly learns to be more demanding and to get its needs met in ever increasing demands until you can deliver no more or take no more abuse.

Everyone recognizes that their lover has a darker side, but most do not question or attempt to work out what impact this will have further into the relationship. An average divorce rate in Western countries of 60 percent testifies to the power of this delusion.(14)

The ego loves plans and has many expectations of how things should be. It cannot tolerate accepting what happens and its main aim is protection of itself. It will see another as someone to gain from. It will view your partner as someone who should do certain things for you. Watch and observe the ego at work being mindful and aware. Should your partner not do what you expect them to do, the ego will criticize them or rob them of self-esteem to build itself up.

The ego has two forms of communication, direct and indirect. If your ego takes the form of anger, then it will be direct when something occurs that is outside its plan for how it should be. You will have seen it operate when road rage occurs. If your ego takes the form of shyness, then it will be indirect.

As an example, a friend had split from her husband and they lived apart for a year. They were having an on/off relationship. She found it difficult to communicate with him to tell him she wanted a divorce. So her ego had her post on Facebook a new relationship and the same day the husband filed for divorce. Her ego knew how he would react. Her ego is running her life in unconsciousness and the result is pain for her also.

Some egos will lie. A male acquaintance was visiting a friend who had recently gone through a divorce. She was feeling very lonely and invited him to stay for dinner. She phoned his wife to ask her to come as well, and told him it was arranged. An hour passed and the wife had not arrived. He phoned his wife and found out she had not agreed to come. His friend's ego had lied about it just to have some company. By listening to her ego, this woman will create deeper loneliness.

If you live in unconsciousness, your ego has you in delusion and it has a plan for you to become further and further deluded, so much so it will create what you seek to avoid.

With relationships, the only solution is for both partners to master awareness and lessen the ego's influence on the relationship and see it for what it is: a spiritual partnership to assist each other to grow the skills and the right level of energy, or vibration, to allow grace to touch their lives.

People come together to learn from each other the missing attributes they need to complete their journey. They may do this over many lifetimes, both now and in the future, until they learn and build their karma for each other.

Where does love fit with the ego?

The divine's love is all encompassing. It is not possessive love in the sense that the divine owns us. The divine is perfection, it is everything, it rests in a state of absolute perfection – and so does that spark in us that is also divine.

The Tao expresses it thus:

It stands alone and alters not.
It revolves eternally without exhaustion.
It is regarded as the Mother of all beings.
I do not know Its name, except to call It Tao.

When forced to give It a name, I would call It "the Great."
The Great is far-reaching.
Far-reaching is infinite.
Infinite is to return to the self-sufficient origin.
Therefore, Tao is great, heaven is great, earth is great, and so is the true-self.
There are four greatness in the universe, and true-self is one of them.(4)

The ego's love, the one you experience most in this world, unfortunately is lacking. Rarely is an individual capable of divine love. Normally, love is given through the ego but only as long as it receives. The ego's love is based on possession of the loved one. It is in the words you listen to in most love songs. You love them because they remind you of the true love that you seek. In the songs there is always the promise of divine love.

A mother's love can be seen as divine if there is no expectation that the child will behave in a particular way. This of course is not realistic because at times you have to discipline the child so it behaves. In the divine there is no such restriction because in that reality there is no expectation or intent to act in any particular way. The way the universe is built ensures that love is compromised by the ego.

In divine love there are no special people; love is distributed equally amongst all. You would love your neighbor as yourself.

In the ego sense, love is used to get from the other. Many relationships disintegrate into two egos serving the needs of the other. When the needs are not met, then the ego will use whatever states or games it has learned to gain back what it perceives it has lost. So it may play games such as victim/dominator or poor me/doormat to gain what it thinks it wants.

The ego does not understand love, nor does it believe in it. It can only see and experience what it understands it to be: a trade for something that will only last this lifetime. It does not understand that through many lives you love certain people and they love you back and support you in your journey.

Often the ego will stay in a relationship even though real love is not present. It can convince that some love, or at least connection to another person, is enough to suffice. The ego will stay in a loveless relationship out of fear.

When you have enough insight and experience, you will view those around you with love and appreciation as they have stayed with you over many lives and you with them.

To break out of the cycle of the ego you must view this relationship and the role it plays in your ultimate journey from a spiritual perspective.

Isn't love the most important thing?

Actually no. The ego would have you believe that, but love is a result of experiencing the truth. Divinity brings love as a natural result of experiencing the truth.

Compassion is therefore the natural response to those caught in ignorance no matter what their actions. That does not mean you allow abuse to occur from those caught in ignorance. However, you can be a compassionate warrior if the need arises. Once you understand that intent is the creator of karma and have experienced the truth, what to do and not do is clear and occurs within you naturally.

There is no debate, only an inner knowing that the divine path will lead you to right actions. Until you are there, this will all be theory and you will approach it from your ego as understanding of what to actions to take. Many will hear this and nod sagely as though understanding. This is the delusion of the ego, which always seeks to swap knowledge for experience.

As quoted from the ancient Hindu Vedas:

> ... *they think that the truth (tattva) regarding Kåñëa* [the divine] *is the mental concoction of certain learned scholars, created by their imaginative brains out of material drawn from the mundane principles.*(15)

Likewise, Lao Tzu said:

A wise man of Tao knows the subtle truth, and may not be learned. A learned person is knowledgeable but may not know the subtle truth of Tao.(4)

Many have given everything for love in a relationship, but this is merely another form of delusion. Love is not something that is given. Love is something that exists and is channelled to another or it is not.

A young woman in her late 20s came to see me about her disastrous relationships with men. A physically beautiful woman, she could have had any man, however she was always attracted to good-looking, cute men who acted like boys. They wanted no commitment and were happy to be in a relationship as long as it didn't interfere with their single man's life. She wondered why this cycle continued.

It eventually became clear to her that the ego had created a false sense of self, portraying her as lacking and needy of men. This pattern had come from her relationship with her father and from previous lives as well. She continually put herself in the inferior position in the relationship. This led to her ego playing the needy role and his ego playing the role of dominator/controller. Her ego was picking the men. It was focusing on his potential and hiding his ego from her.

She had noticed he was always out with the boys, but her ego would respond "That's just what men do" and she could easily believe this because all the men her ego selected had behaved that way, based on the model of her father. So to her it was normality. It was her reality even if it was not the reality. Her ego made her look at who they could be. The reality she could not see was their ego was in the way and resistant to change.

This man didn't want to change. His ego tried to bring her back into the relationship after they had parted numerous times, even promising that he would do whatever it took including going to counselling. She was overjoyed, but when it came time to live up to the promise, he always had an excuse. The ego would speak to her and say things like "You just need to work harder at this, it's not really his fault, you are hard work to be with." It was only after meditation and self-awareness arose that she began to separate the ego from herself and could see the delusion of what it had been offering her.

She eventually broke free from the ego's grip and the relationship. The relationship wasn't the lesson, freedom from the ego was.

A relationship can be a great tool to spiritual freedom. It can be seen for what it really is and used as a form of *awakening* to bring your awareness to higher levels. The special relationship that the ego has can be turned into the special spiritual relationship that reveals more about you than you could learn anywhere else.

I'm confused. Are you saying that we should give up everything? Our houses, joyful emotions, fun, drink and even working and just seek to awaken?

No. There are many things that you have created that are indeed inspired by your true nature of divinity. A child's smile, a beautiful sunset, a rose opening. A heartfelt conversation with a friend.

Enjoying life doesn't pull you away from *awakening*. Being led by the ego to fixate on any one thing does. It may be a behavior, money, drugs, smoking, sex, violence, laziness, appearing a certain way to others – it really is all the same to the ego. Most of you have fallen into something that is called being unaware. This is what the ego wants.

There is a profound difference between sitting watching a sunset with your mind thinking and altering the experience and watching it with no ego filter.

It's like watching a movie through dark glasses. You still see the same images but the richness is missing. Some may describe life as grey or dull. Others will not notice it. One day after the next, it's all the same. Most describe *awakening* as seeing the brightness of colors for the first time. They see better, hear clearer, feel more.

After *awakening* you will still do the same things, but you will experience the world very differently from before. *Awakening* is not giving anything up, it is adding to the richness of life. The ego will tell you that you are giving up you. It will say that you are losing something. Once you *awaken* you will know that the false you you have lived for many years is gone.

Most of you cannot retire from the world and seek to *awaken*. You must do it within your daily lives. You must find time to set aside for the practices.

The ego will say there is not enough time. However, the truth is that there is always the time if you want it.

I have a friend who is bubbly all the time. She does not seem to have an ego.

Everyone's ego is different. Being bubbly doesn't mean a person does not have one. They are still influenced by it.

Being too positive has its downside. The ego will ensure that positive people don't see issues or problems when they arise and that they are not able to respond to emotional problems with empathy or insight. This is generally the pattern that is used. However, they still require *awakening* to occur.

It can be more difficult to discern the ego's impact in such people as it projects to others any negatives. As it focuses only on the positive, anyone who brings problems will be seen as the enemy trying to bring them down. The ego can even go further to say they are jealous of the other's positivity.

The ego in this instance is using a pattern it has developed to focus only on the positive and ignore the pain, particularly emotional pain. If emotional issues need to be discussed, then it does not want to as it involves feeling pain and focusing on what is not going well. The filtering of the ego will not allow that.

If your ego is like this, the solution is to have awareness of the ego. Begin to separate it from you. Come down off the false high of the ego. Become more human and more in touch with your heart and your real emotions. You are then able to share these with others.

Now touched by the divine you will be able to address the real events that are happening and not the ego's filtered version of them.

If you have a friend with an ego like this, you can assist by bringing awareness to them initially, then in further depth in an *awakening* to how their ego has them deluded.

What if I feel sad all the time?

You may have also asked yourself the question: "Why do I feel tired, anxious and depressed all the time?"

Sadness, like all ego-inspired negative emotions, is born from one of three sources: parental patterning, events, and your culture.

The ego will use any of these as the basis for patterns that occur in your life. The patterns are there to recognize a threat. That threat can be a lack of attention or a lack of love. Perhaps you experienced embarrassment as a child, disconnection from a parent, striving for success, domination by an adult, another's abuse. In such cases, the ego will set up a pattern to avoid it occurring again. However, this pattern will ensure you experience it constantly. If you experienced embarrassment, it may call you shy and ensure that during social gatherings you will be the wallflower hiding away in the corner, thereby avoiding embarrassment. Or you will act embarrassed, ensuring you draw attention to yourself as socially inept.

If you observed direct or subtle family messages that success meant value, worth and love, then you will begin to constantly strive to achieve. This will be to avoid a feeling of being left out of the family group because what is valued in your family is success.

As an adult, the ego will set in place a pattern that constantly has you in busy mode and seeking status and success. As you gain more, then more will be required. This is the most basic of the ego's strategies. The consequence of this pattern will be less time available for social relationships. These will suffer and you will eventually experience loneliness – the very emotion you were seeking to avoid when you were young.

Disconnection from a parent, such as a father from a daughter, can create a pattern of constantly seeking to obtain the father's love through many men. The ego, though, is choosing men who will treat you the way you have become patterned to believe it should be. The men you choose will not return your love because what your ego gives them is neediness and this is repellant to a man. They will eventually leave as, no matter what they do, they can never take away your fear that they will leave. This cycle of relationships is evident in many young women today.

The father may have left or was never there emotionally, so the ego pattern is to find a man who will not be present and eventually leave. It is sad to see so many women unable to maintain a relationship that will bring them support. Again, what the ego seeks to avoid, it will create by the pattern it sets up.

Each of these patterns has the one ultimate purpose in the thinking of the ego: to protect you. The reality is that what you are seeking to avoid the ego will bring to you. Its thinking is flawed and always will be.

You would have adopted these patterns when you were quite young and now your ego will use them to keep you in fear of being hurt, but will cause you to miss out on leading a full life. It will lessen your expectations about life. Okay will be enough. Rather than try, most people would rather experience okay so there is no risk. This is the ego's plan.

You can break out of this cycle by *awakening*. This is a divine purpose and one worthy of you. Once awake, the sadness will be like a dream of a past life. There as a distant memory.

How do I call others to awaken? I live and work with some people who drive me crazy and need to hear this!

Once you are *awakened*, Buddha said the correct reaction to the delusion of others is compassion.

It is only your ego that reacts and compares and seeks to separate you from them by its reaction. The divine in you knows and can see that it is only their misinterpretation of reality that causes them to act the way they do. They mean no harm but, unchecked, their ego will cause harm to themselves and to you.

Compassion does not mean you allow abuse to you or others to occur. That would merely teach the ego that it is permissible. If they continue their behavior, you must leave. If you don't, then your ego has become involved. It seeks to join with their ego and draw on the negative energy created.

If they wish to argue, you must withdraw and observe their behavior in the same manner as you would observe your own negative thoughts.

Move to a higher level of consciousness. Become more *awake* and see clearly what their ego is trying to achieve. Has it been triggered by a pattern? Are they lonely or hurt? If you cannot respond and calm it, then withdraw and disengage from it.

To stay will allow your own ego to become engaged. Once you reach higher levels of *awakening*, your own light of consciousness will shine and its peace will influence them to respond in the same way.

That's why in a master's presence you feel the calmness and peace that emanates from them.

Until that occurs for you, you can discuss with them what you have learnt about yourself and the truth. They may seek to know more. If they do not, then you may have to wait until they are in enough pain to want to hear you. Alternatively, something may occur that will cause them to have a moment of clarity, of awareness, and then they may wish to respond.

Your purpose should be to *awaken* yourself and then become the light for others to follow.

How can I raise my children with awareness?

Jesus said, "Be as little children." He was referring to the egoless state that children live in most of the time. They are present to the present. As Eckhart Tolle said in his book, *The Power of Now*, being present can hold the ego at bay.(13) Another way of saying that is to rest in the divine.

Being in the present is being at one with the divine. The divine is in the present moment as that is all there is. Eternity is the present moment. In that moment the ego does not exist. The ego only exists in the past or the future where it would have you live.

Children have that mastered. That is not to say they don't have an ego at times; however, it is not yet fully engaged to the collective ego or fully developed in their personal ego. They tend to be in that egoless state when they play. They are fully absorbed in what they are doing and very present.

In moments with them, when they are caught in their ego, you can discuss the ego and what it is. Awareness initially comes through knowledge.

Educating your children in what it is becomes the foundation of their freedom from it. Once they can recognize when their ego is speaking to them, then they have the tools to break free.

If you seek to raise your children with awareness of the ego, you must become aware of its influence on your relationship with them. The ego will use your love for your children for its own purpose. It will smother them too much and rob them of their independence. The ego will try to tell them how they should live their lives and make them an extension of your own life. It will react badly when they try to exert independence and it will keep you too busy to devote the time to them. Time is a child's currency; it shows them by your actions that you care for and love them.

They will model your ego and it will show them how to carry on the same patterns of the ego that do not work for you. They will inherit the negative from you, just because they model you.

It will not be a hindrance, however, if you refer to the ego every time they do something wrong. When they have finished their tantrum and calmed, then speak to them of the mechanics of how the ego operates. Teach them to become aware of the moment of truth when awareness *awakens*.

However, be aware when you speak to your children with your ego, either in pride or anger. Do not allow your ego have them see you as perfect because they can never live up to that expectation the ego is planting in them.

Teach your children self-esteem and to expect to be treated fairly and spoken to appropriately.

Help them to separate their true nature from the false one the ego would have them adopt. Be aware that the patterned conditioning and modeling of the ego begins to operate more intensively from puberty onwards. There is a change in the consciousness at around this age as the child consciousness fades and is replaced by the adult ego, separation.

This practice alone can awaken them to be more conscious of the ego and speed their journey to *awaken*. This is your ultimate role as a parent. To speed the journey of their soul to the divine.

How does the ego work in families?

Never well. The divine, however, always works beautifully.

The ego will always hide the truth from you. If it is active, it will favor one child over the other and hide awareness of its action from you. The result will be sibling rivalry to gain equal attention.

It may cause you to become too busy and neglect giving real attention to your children. Time is their currency measure of love. If you spend enough one-on-one time with them, they know they are loved. If you become distracted and fail to, the ego has won.

The ego can also make you too rigid and too serious with your children. It can make you angry and respond harshly, losing their respect. One child may reflect back to you the ego patterns you cannot observe in yourself and this will make your ego angry. It will respond harshly and treat this child unfairly.

The divine wants to teach children about their own ego so they can recognize yours and know when they are not being treated appropriately. The divine knows that you are all one and that you have come together to lift each other to awareness. When a family is viewed from that perspective, the ego's delusion is lessened.

The ego always uses events in childhood to blame you. If abuse occurs, the child's ego will take the blame itself. The thought will be "They treat me like this because there is something wrong with me". That pattern can last many years until the truth can be seen by them.

The primary purpose that any family is together is to assist each other to reach an *awakening*. Your love and commitment can assist your children to grow into *awakened* souls.

How do I seek to become *awakened* when there are so many practical things to do each day?

Buddha once said, "The ordinary man will find it very difficult to find enlightenment."(1) What he meant was that amidst the day-to-day obligations it can be difficult to find the time to devote to finding the truth. That doesn't mean it's impossible.

There are times when you can focus on what you need to do without thought. If you step back to observe yourself you will see that most "thoughts" mean nothing and you can carry out most tasks without thinking because you already know what you need to do. Thought does not tell you what you need to do next, it only comments on what you do. Even learning a new skill doesn't need to involve thought or, expressed another way, talking to yourself. All talking is the ego.

Your real self, your consciousness, inhabits your body, and for good reason the heart is called the seat of the soul. When you follow your heart, there is a sense of being on the right path, being guided to do the right thing. That sense is expressed as a body sensation.

Consider an emotion. What is it? It is not a chemical reaction in your brain; it may begin there but it is "felt" in the body and these feelings are universal. You feel fear in your stomach, joy in your heart, excitement in your throat and chest. It is through these sensations that you know what you feel.

When you are trusting and have to deal with day-to-day decisions, there is a sense, a knowing, an intuition of what to do.

All creative people know this space. Some describe it as "in the flow"; there is no thought, just perfection. The Japanese practice it in martial arts, painting, the tea ceremony and sword fighting. Its foundation is in Zen. You can have Zen every day! But be aware that Zen is not a goal just a path pointing to the truth. It involves minimal thought and doing what you need to do.

This will not happen without practice and in practice you must have a base of belief that you can build on, meaning practice for practice sake will not bring you closer to the truth. Practice with a base of experience of reaching closer to the divine and knowing the truth will.

The ultimate practice is to become *awakened*, which means being free of the ego and bringing your consciousness out of the background into the foreground and experiencing your meditative state every day doing what you normally do.

I have a business. How can I run it in accord with these principles?

You must live and work in the world whilst allowing time for quiet moments with the divine.

Losing yourself in business is one of the easiest ways to avoid the truth. Buddha worked with many rich princes who found it difficult to give full attention to the truth. Wealth is a great distraction. Jesus said:

> *Truly, I say to you, only with difficulty, will a rich person enter the kingdom of heaven.(7)*

The Tao Te Ching says:

When success is achieved, he seeks no recognition.
Because he does not claim for the credit, hence shall not lose it.(4)

You can incorporate the truth and this way of viewing the world in anything you do, from walking the street and doing the dishes to running your business. Find the experience of the truth for yourself, and then you will know clearly how to incorporate it into your business. Realize there are no coincidences and that those you meet, including clients and team members, are part of your journey home, and become aware of the lessons you can learn from each other and their impact.

Run your business with no ego. Run it with purpose and operate it for the team that works in it and the customers it serves and your business will thrive.

The why of the business, if in alignment with the divine, will attract to it, those who seek the same.

Create a culture in your business that promotes that connection and interchange. Not just with those who work for you but with your customers. Your business can be your vehicle to live the truth fully, and then you will be in a position to influence many by creating a culture that promotes the truth.

How will this help with depression?

Depression is a lack of meaning. It is the result of not having any belief outside of yourself. It can be changed by experiencing a moment of divinity and realizing that you are the creator of your experience.

Depression is the ego's way of using your body against you. It has a set sequence of allowing your body to alter your physiology so as to enter the state known as depression. Your mind then becomes cloudy and lacks focus, and your energy vibrates at a very slow level, attracting more negative energy.

Watch someone who is depressed. Do they move fast or slow?

Watch their breath. They have become practiced at slowing it down. Ask them about their thoughts. You will find they are all negative because they are living mostly at the ego's vibration level and the only voice they hear is the ego's. There is no balance. That's why exercise can assist; it changes the vibration level of their energy and hence their physiology.

If you wish to move away from depression, learn to be still, focus and move towards the divine. Once awareness comes, depression leaves, because under the light of awareness darkness cannot stand. Depression is darkness disguised as a disease.

If you suffer from depression, you will know of what I speak. Jim Carrey suffered many years until he chose to *awaken* to what was really missing in his life. Real meaning, based on the truth. Robin Williams unfortunately did not *awaken*.

Standing in the truth, depression does not exist. It can only be present in states of the ego, not states of the divine. When you move into ego states, you may access the state you call depression. When you are with the divine, depression as a state in that plane does not exist. You will not be able to access it.

To the ego, depression serves a purpose. It gains the ego attention, it gives it something to focus on that appears out of its control and hence you cannot focus on anything else. It overwhelms your life to ensure you remain stuck.

A large portion of the planet is now on antidepressants. They alter your brain chemistry to allow you to find a stable place from which to recover. Meditation and mindfulness have been shown to be very beneficial for depression sufferers.(16)

Become aware, move to *awaken*, and you will leave this and many other forms of suffering behind.

I'm always stressed. I can't ever seem to calm down. I'm always out partying, chasing a good time. How can you help me?

You must question why you won't set aside time to put spiritual practices in place in your life. Ask the question: "Why won't my ego let me calm down?" Contemplate this during a meditation and await what answer arises.

Listen to the voice, become calm, hear what it says to you. Feel the compulsion to always be doing something, never allowing yourself to be with yourself.

The ego sets up this strategy to run from yourself, making you believe that if you stop you will not like what you find, so better to keep busy and keep running. Nothing could be further from the truth. It is in peace that you see and experience who you really are. Not the apparition the ego would have you believe is you.

The ego always wants to keep you busy so you don't stop, because when you do, you will become more aware and begin to separate the real you, the truth, from your ego. As that begins to happen, the stress and the busy life will cease.

An essential practice is to slow down, to find moments for yourself. Leave the office during the day and sit quietly on a park bench. Rise an hour earlier in the morning. Stay up later at night. Go inside to find your connection.

Busyness can become an addiction and one that the ego loves because it keeps a veil over the truth. It is only in stillness that you can begin the process of reaching it.

I am just getting by and need to put food on the table. I don't have time to meditate or devote myself to this.

That is fine. There is no time limit. At some point, though, you will face the same challenge.

Instilling in yourself a sense of peace and calm will ensure you have time. It's not that the time doesn't exist, it's that you make it not exist for you. Your ego ensures you do not have the time to devote to being free.

If you closely examine your life, you will experience the pressure you are under just living in this world.

You may say you feel under pressure all the time, but when you stop, truly stop, you will see that there is more pressure than you acknowledge.

That acknowledgment will be the door to the light. That moment of thought, away from the ego, can be built on. That moment can turn into awareness and in that awareness a seed can be planted – and *awakening* can now blossom.

You rush through your lives without peace. There is only one moment of peace and that is outside the ego's constructs of past and future. The only time you can be, is right now. That moment is when your life gets better.

If you chase *awakening* to make your life better, it is merely the ego deluding you again. Instead of chasing money or time to relax or prestige or glory or fast cars, now you are chasing *awakening*. That is a trap.

Awakening is your ultimate journey.

I never seem to get the success I'm chasing, it's always eluding me.

Not achieving success and wealth is not what you fear. You are allowing your ego to have control of your life, to strive for goals it thinks are important because its perspective is of one life and it needs to have it all in this one.

The ego offers success as a goal. However, this is a poor substitute for what you really are and want. This will never satisfy. Those who have achieved it will testify that, once it is obtained, the ego moves to the next person, marriage, car or the thing that will become the "new" goal.

This becomes a never-ending cycle of objects, none of which will provide any lasting joy. The only way out of the cycle is to find the truth for yourself. You can still have these things, secure in the truth that you don't need them or want them but can still enjoy them.

The ego will not be able to use them to create havoc in your life because of what you possess, and negative karma will cease.

Abundance will follow.

Is it wrong to have money, wear nice clothes, possess things?

You have to live in this world and the level of possessions is not the question. It is your focus and obsession with them that matters.

There is nothing intrinsically wrong with possessions. However, the ego will become involved in owning anything until you *awaken*. Your culture now has an egoic obsession with possessing things, convincing you that these things are part of you and hence make "you" more acceptable, more recognized, more loved. The ego's mantra is buy more stuff you don't need and you will be someone.

The truth is you are someone already.

So many young girls today are pressured into being what they are not. Because they feel they can't live up to these perfect ideals of what a woman should be, they become lost, some resorting to self-harm or suicide, both of which are all too prevalent in Western society.

Some say they are seeking to find themselves but they are still seeking an empty version of the real self. An ego-inspired self that is centered on one thing, the ego.

The true self is one based in the divine. A self that can only be found in the truth.

Lao Tzu said in the Tao:

> *Tao is so profound and yet is invisible, It exists in everywhere and anywhere.*
> *I do not know whose Son It is, It existed before heaven and earth.*(4)

Have a nice home, a nice car, but focus on finding the truth. From that will come balance. You will want to help others because you know you are all one. Don't try to help first because the ego will take ownership of what a good person you are through a value it holds of doing the right thing. That is not the truth.

There is intrinsically no right or wrong in the possession of things, it's in the ego's use of these things to make you lose yourself in the desire to have them before being balanced in yourself. Having possessions whilst living in the truth is different from possessing things and being attached to them. Attachment takes the form of "These things add to who I am. Look at what I own." Or "Having these things will make me feel good."

First experience the truth, then live in this world with a balanced view of possessions.

Won't I need practical skills as well? Like how to run a business, how to maintain a relationship?

Yes, if you wish to find balance in this life, other knowledge will need to be acquired.

In the special relationship, you must know how the masculine and feminine states work, to find balance and provide what your partner seeks. In most relationships today these are out of balance. The Yin and Yang are confused. She is in the Yang and he is in the Yin. This causes disharmony and dissatisfaction.

The Tao states:

> *To know the strong masculine principle, yet abide by the gentle female principle is like being the valley of the world where all rivers will flow into.*
> *This is alike all virtue which will merge into the subtle Tao.(4)*

The feminine needs the masculine in the relationship so it can feel safe and have a soft place to rest. The masculine used in the correct way is not dominating, destructive or violent. That is the ego. The true masculine nature is in alignment with the divine and has purpose and certainty, and holds the feminine in its safety. It protects and nurtures and provides what the feminine needs – true support emotionally.

The primary cause of so many relationship failures and why one-third of all births are now to single mothers in Western countries is the ego dominating in the relationship. For many women a relationship seems too difficult.

If the relationship exists for its correct purpose – to share an *awakening* not just with each other but with many – then the relationship shifts and changes.

Unfortunately, divorce rates are between 42 and 70 percent in Western countries.(14) This trend is caused by the respective egos having a relationship with each other. This can be avoided if the purpose of the relationship is clear from the beginning. When a relationship is inspired by the divine and directed to the divine, then the ego is contained.

As for operating a business, the same principle applies. Marketing, team and operational skills are required for today's careers. Performing those skills *awakened* provides a very different experience and result.

Businesses that are *awakened* have a strong strategy that is divinely inspired and that the organization is moved to implement. Those businesses seek to do good and no harm. They make profit but that is a byproduct of their purpose. Customers and the team rally to the intent, the why, the cause.

Awakening is an essential ingredient of any business and any relationship.

It seems impossible to always do good. What about crushing an ant?

Intent is what counts. Negative karma is attracted by intent. If you listen to the ego and follow its suggested actions, you attract negative karma. Please do not be deluded by this.

We are not talking about Divine retribution. The divine does not know retribution. The concept of Divine retribution came about through early pagan beliefs, the Old Testament and the Christian tradition. The divine does not seek retribution. However, the ego will create and attract negativity, so the more negativity you create, the more you receive. That may appear in a false belief system to be retribution.

If your intention is to harm the ant and bring pain, then negative karma is created by the state you are in, not by the act itself. If you are laying out ant killer because the ants are overrunning your house, there is no negative karma.

If you kill in anger, there is. If you kill to defend your country or your family, there is not. Intent is what's important. If you defend your country through peaceful discussion or protest, even more positive karma is created.

However, be aware, only the ego would seek positive karma for reward. Your divine nature attracts it because that is what it is. Gandhi, for example, was able to master himself to be in the divine, thus becoming one of the great leaders of the 20th century.

Let me state clearly, though, negative karma should not be your concern, just as positive karma should not be your goal. It is only the ego that wants to keep score.

If you experience the truth, you will not be concerned about anything. Negative karma is not a concept that will hold any focus for you.

If you have not experienced the truth as yet, negative karma is merely something that is part of delusion.

All it means is that it keeps you from the truth and adds to the delusion. Negative karma is best viewed as roadblocks on the path to experiencing the truth.

I live a good life and am happy with my life. Why do I need this?

In any life there are challenges.

There are things about yourself that you know can be improved. It may be communication with others, or habits that don't serve you and others, or moments of poor mood, or decisions that could have been better.

Eventually this life or another will be disrupted by the ego. At that moment you will need this. These experiences will bring you home. Now or later, that choice is yours. Observe carefully, every life has a leveler. That is the way of this universe. You must live within its laws.

Many seek to live a quiet and safe life. However, life karma has a way of disrupting that plan. When it does, who do you blame? How do you make sense of it? It's just luck? Or randomness?

Consider carefully: on the surface the universe can appear random, but everything has order and laws. Your life is the same. You are subject to them whether you acknowledge it or not.

Even those who appear to have it all have their challenges. Life has levelers. Negative karma is attracted when you ignore the truth and remain in ignorance.

That negative karma comes through your life in many ways. The ego operates within your life whether you acknowledge it or not. You will make a decision, your ego will have influenced that decision, and it will result in major disruption even for those who feel they live and have lived a good life.

How do I help a friend who is living in their ego all the time?

The ego is never ready to listen to the truth.

You can only wait for a moment of awareness arising for your friend. Sometimes the divine brings events that can prompt awareness. A loss of some type can be a tragedy or it can become a moment of awareness. If your friend can hold the awareness, then they will see there is something to take from the loss.

Every event can be used for delusion or awareness. That decision is influenced by their karmic journey as to the level of motivation they have to be aware and the events in this life that prompt them to maintain that awareness.

If you wish to assist your friend, you may choose the right moment when you can feel awareness present in them. Begin by drawing to their attention the results they are currently achieving and that they are not what they really want. You can then explain the ego to them so they can distinguish who they are listening to. You may find they have little awareness about the results. They may think it's all fine, but others around them notice what is really happening.

A wealthy couple was in this situation. She had a child from another marriage and two from their own. He was very busy with his business and she was busy with her fitness, working out every day. He treated her child differently from the other two. It was obvious to her but not to him.

She liked to keep the peace so said little. He, having no awareness of his behavior, saw the situation as normal. His ego would not let him see reality – not until a conversation with her brought awareness. This is always the first step to *awakening*.

If your friend is not ready to listen, then you must be patient until an opportunity arises. If an event occurs that forces awareness around the result of living in the ego, then they may listen.

It may be difficult to watch as they create results they don't actually want; however, compassion is the correct response until they are ready to hear the message.

I'm in a relationship and we have two children and I can't decide whether to stay or go. It's not that he's unkind, I just can't decide if I should leave?

Whenever you have to make a decision, you can be sure the ego is involved.

You often chase "love" when going from one partner to another. That is not the solution. When you acknowledge from experience that you are with the people around you for eternity, you will see the situation from a different perspective. He or she may not be exciting you at the moment. That will generally be due to your ego having set this up after the honeymoon period ended in your relationship.

During the honeymoon period you are really "in divine love" – you see nothing of the faults of the other, you see only the best. Then it changes and the ego begins to look for fault to keep itself from being hurt. But soon there is a brick wall of faults from both partners from things you have done to each other, and the ego remembers them all.

It does not forgive. Its logic is, if you let them get away with them, then they will take advantage of you. It cannot see that its own distorted communication is causing most of the problems. Most relationships fail because of misunderstandings. It's not that the partners don't love each other, it's merely they don't experience the love anymore.

Withheld love can be felt by your partner without anything being spoken. Love is truly an energy that each of you can feel. It is palpable when it is present and so it can be sent to or withheld from the other. When even a little is withheld, the other will do the same. Then communication comes not from love but from the ego which is trying to get. The other feels it and withdraws into the ego as well. Now the relationship is dominated by two egos attempting to get. The ego does not believe in love, it only understands taking and getting what it needs. That is its form of love.

This is a recipe for failure. To use your relationship for its true purpose of bringing you closer to the divine, remove the ego with awareness.

The relationship will then serve its best purpose, to raise you up and fill your hearts with the love that is your right. It's no longer about what you can take but what you give.

My life seems to be spiraling out of control. I lost my business and the current one isn't working either. My marriage is failing. What can I do to bring back my mojo?

You have been listening to the ego. At some point in your journey you have strayed from what you knew was the right thing to do. The ego's plan is always to protect you. However, it uses its store of negative behaviors to find a plan which is flawed from the beginning. So, if you say you want something more, it will look outside the relationship for something better.

The problem is that allowing the ego to guide you in the search for something better is like giving a torch to a shark in murky waters and expecting it not to eat you. The ego will select the new and improved body for you to be with. So your ego will select their ego rather than connect to their divine. Now two egos will have a relationship. The ending is predictable even if the timing is not.

To remove yourself from this cycle, you must raise your awareness and cease listening to the ego. Connecting to your divine will allow you to be guided by true knowledge to find a path that is far easier than the ego's.

I just want to live happily and be free from this voice in my head. This seems all too hard.

Everyone will find their own way out of the pain that is part of life. Some seem to attract more pain than others. That is karma, but it is also choice. Karma sets the base for your circumstances but you have free choice to choose a different way. Many have been born into families or circumstances where they experienced abuse, but arose from that to do great things.

Others pretend they live happily, but at times are tortured by the ego. It will tell them to do something and then criticize them for having done it. It can only do that by talking to them.

If there are strong voices in your head, firstly realize that we all have voices in our head. Secondly, realize that you focus on them rather than focus externally on life, and thirdly, that you have a choice not to listen to them and to focus instead on the beauty of life. Don't be trapped by "wanting" the external, but at the same time focus on life's beauty and that is what life will become for you. You can focus on the dark or the light, the choice is yours.

Focus on not listening to the ego's voice as it speaks rather than listening to the voice which you used to believe was you. Mindfulness in that moment will catch the thought before you grasp it as your own. In that second of awareness you can capture the thought and identify it as being of the ego.

Separate you from the voice. That is the first part of the practice to begin your journey. The second is to become more aware when the ego in you reacts to things that occur. Focus on the positive events and turn off the tap of fear that the ego likes to keep running. If you identify with it, you will experience constant fear, which is what most experience every moment –fear created by the ego which focuses on the past and future rather than the present moment.

Focus determines what you hear and see. This is a path to freedom out of that trap. The voice that says "It's too hard" is the ego's.

I'm always chasing something, always searching for something. I'm not clear on what it is, but I'm afraid it's just another dead end.

At times you will have an ache inside that yearns for greater certainty that the divine and love are real. It can at times seem distant. No amount of thinking, searching or mental gymnastics over the existence of the divine will make it real to you. You can allow your ego to debate as much as it likes over what the divine is and how it operates in this world, it will not change the fact, the divine is the truth.

The ego will never let you rest. It wants to keep you busy and running. Its fear is that you will be still for a moment and experience a connection. If you do feel the need inside to have time to feel that connection, you may express this to yourself as "I'm so tired, I just need to stop."

However, saying that doesn't make you stop and use the teachings and the practice. The only way you will know it's true is to have an experience of the divine yourself. Even if you are ready, as you seek to find it, you will experience many dead ends. The ego will take you down many of these roads as it is fearful of you disengaging from it. When its power weakens, it dies. It can only exist as the opposite of what is true.

The divine is true peace and love and exists within you as a natural extension of its peace. It is that feeling of utter stability and peace that you seek so that no matter what happens, you can be at peace with the event. The ego seeks never-ending thought and busyness so you have no time to think of the truth. If you are not, it will use guilt or responsibility to manipulate you into being busy.

Awareness is to see clearly how the ego works. This leads to *awakening*.

How do I keep my body clean and light?

If you have ever observed someone in the grips of depression or anxiety, their state is one of heaviness or frantic energy. There is no peace. Their diet also reflects how they feel. Their bodies are heavy and frantic.

It is not a precondition of *awakening* to eat in any particular way. Rather, moving to *awaken* you will want to eat less, fast more and generally not overindulge in anything, including food.

As a patient becomes healthy, they look better, walk with a lighter step and smile more. They eat, rest and sleep appropriately.

Overeating is a sign of the ego having control. There is dissatisfaction with life and boredom. Eating fills that gap. Once you know the truth you will not feel like overeating. The more you move to the divine, the more you will want life-giving light food and you will be inspired to keep your body fit and young.

Have you noticed how those who are spiritually inspired tend to age slower than most. They look younger than their years. Their bodies do not show the signs of holding the ego's pain in them. They have cleared the pain and their bodies are light, and brightness shines from their eyes whatever their age.

How do I use this in my search for my soul mate?

Your soul mate will find you. You travel many lives and many journeys. In these you share many with the same souls. They come to assist you and to help you find your way back. You also assist them or hold them back depending on where you are in your own journey. The purpose of meeting again is to finish what was started.

If you are referring to a lover, that relationship can be either the best or the worst for your journey. Finding the right partner is also about *awakening* to the true purpose of the relationship, which is to assist each other to move more to the divine.

The ego's idea of a relationship is to use it for getting. The true purpose of your soul mate is someone who is serving their purpose in the interconnectedness designed to *awaken* you from your sleep. You meet many people designed for that purpose and guided by the divine to assist you to become more, grow and experience who you really are.

Your soul mate is not someone special, as the ego would have them be. They are someone who is karmically with you to assist you to grow. That is true love.

Viewed from this standpoint you will have more tolerance and appreciation of them for being with you.

Does personal development or psychology help?

You can solve a relationship pattern or lose weight or create wealth for yourself using these methods, but the ego will use your times of unawareness to create further patterns that bring unhappiness.

Whilst these methodologies are useful, they do not solve the underlying essential issue, which is to *awaken*. Many spend their lives seeking answers in experiences and searching for a truth. The key is to observe that over centuries other masters have trodden the same path as you. They point the way. It is clear there is one journey.

Personal development may bring you closer to the point of wanting to *awaken*, so it has a use from that perspective. The ego, however, can use this knowledge to hide behind or delude you in the search.

Being pious does not mean you are *awake*. Jesus spoke of this in relation to the Pharisees:

> *You're nothing but show-offs. You lock people out of the kingdom of heaven. You won't go in yourselves, and you keep others from going in.*(7)

If you constantly talk about what you have achieved on the search and tell others how to live, you can be sure it is your ego speaking. Personal development can be a tool to lead toward *awakening* but it is not *awakening*.

Some teaching is not revealing of the truth and you must decide for yourself if this is so. If you connect to the divine, that decision will be clear to you. The ego, however, will attempt to use it for its own purposes. It will use your knowledge to keep the truth hidden from you by focusing on the tools rather than the destination.

Does this bring great wealth?

The search for great wealth is ego inspired and leads to increasing ignorance. Equally, there is nothing intrinsically wrong with accumulating great wealth.

It is when the desire for great wealth becomes an addiction and is ego inspired that darkness descends. Unawareness follows at a cost to this life and the next unless it is undone by using the wealth wisely.

The purpose of *awakening* is not to become rich. That may be a byproduct of that choice, but it is not its purpose. The path attracts good karma and it includes wealth, but not as a reward or even as a result of focus, a goal or action taken. Rather, good energy follows good energy.

The Tao says:

> *Therefore, the saint always conducts himself with the essence of Tao and never departs from It.*
> *Although he is surrounded by the splendor of wealth, he remains to live a simple and ordinary life.(4)*

Money is really just a promise that I will do something or give something to you. The more you do and provide, "the more your cup will overflow", to quote Jesus.

So choose to *awaken* because it is your ultimate journey and rewards far greater will follow.

Will my life be blissful?

Your life will be less eventful. Calmer, more peaceful, but blissful no. That word is reserved for moments of grace. They do not last. Only in the divine does bliss last.

Each day will be like all others except you will walk with a clear step with surety of purpose, knowing that you are secure. Bliss means to ignore reality. With *awakening* you are living in the moment, without filters, experiencing life as it is rather than filtered and altered. There is great joy in the experience.

Bliss in this universe tends to denote an unreality, a disconnection from what is real. Nothing in *awakening* is further from the truth. Seeking bliss is also a distraction and delusion. The experience of bliss will not bring you to the truth. You may experience bliss on the journey, but do not seek it as the destination.

How do I know what to think and what to follow? How can I know the truth for myself and not rely on you or anyone?

Buddha exhorted his students to find their own way. It is excellent advice.

When you have the experience of connecting to the divine through meditation or a spontaneous event generated by correct preparation and karma, you will know for yourself what is true.

Studying books can point you in the correct direction but it will not set you free. It provides a background from which to launch yourself into *awakening*.

Initially, and depending on your level of karma, you will need guidance. The ego has many delusions, and guidance is necessary not to be trapped. Hence the centuries old tradition of the master and student in Buddhism and the priest and his flock in Christianity.

These guides are there to point you in the correct direction as you shed your negative karma, build your positive karma and reduce reliance on patterns the ego holds. You will come to a point when the only journey left is inwards.

Your guide will shorten time for you, saving many years of endless paths on the road. You may spend years meditating but still be no closer to the truth. You may read all the ancient texts and still not approach it. You may travel the world in search of the best master and still not arrive. These are not the ways to obtain grace.

There is a set path. Vary from it and you will become lost in the ego. You must find your own way to the divine eventually, but do not attempt to do it on your own. That path is the ego, which needs nothing and no one.

Once your guide has shown you the path forward, you must rely on the map you have been given as you leave the shore. Once on the ocean, where you end up will be determined by how strongly you can hold the rudder.

This is now reliant on you and your control of your mind and your heart's desire to *awaken*. The power of your concentration to hold true to the course you must follow.

Are all negative emotions the ego?

Every negative emotion is ego based. The ego is about separation and every negative emotion from fear to jealousy or shyness is about separation.

There are over 3500 emotions and most of these are negative. Peace, joy, love are inherently part of the divine. The peace we experience here is not the same as the peace of the divine. Its peace is absolute. It is perfection and total ecstasy. There is nothing in this universe that can compare to it.

The ego has no concept of this and uses far weaker emotions to keep you amused and to give variety to an otherwise meaningless existence. It knows that if you are still, you will remember where you came from and who you are. So it is always keeping you thinking, doing things, experiencing emotions and dealing with self-made problems. Problems like fighting in a relationship, complaining about your work, arguing with a child, worrying about money, whining that the dishes weren't done last night.

These comments and critiques that the ego offers are believed by you. You think this is you saying these things, but it is not. It is your ego.

Whenever you are criticizing, that is your ego. It is separating them from you. That's why Jesus said:

> Why do you see the speck that is in your brother's eye, but do not notice the log that is in your own eye?(7)

By criticising, the ego creates separation. It's them and you. Instead of the truth that we are all one. By separation, the ego keeps itself alive in you. You can hear it in the stillness. Once you master listening, you can hear it every moment saying something about others or yourself.

The filter it uses is false. It is delusion.

I meditate, I spend time with myself, I want to reach the divine and be free but I still seem stuck.

The ego's mechanism of striving for something, then when you do not reach it using it to punish you with internal criticism, is its basic mechanism of defense to prevent you from connecting to the divine.

The object of your desire is now to reach this place. This place of peace and connection. This is the ego striving for something; it is making a goal from your desire. When you can do the practice without the need for an outcome, then you will arrive.

The ego must divert you. Its structure will collapse if it does not. It will use thoughts during your practice to pull you away from concentration. During meditation, when a thought arises and you allow it to take hold, you will be swept away with it. At some point you must wake up and come back to concentration. This will happen many times until you break through the primary veil of delusion and know that this has occurred.

Piercing the veil is where you will experience the peace.

Be aware. If you focus on the peace you hold within, it cannot be taken from you by the ego or anything else. This is your birth right. Rest in it, float in it. Approach the practice with the peace held firmly within and with no expectation because that is the ego arising. Approach it with peace, and no expectation of a result, just pure concentration, pure awareness.

Life should be approached this way as well. Life should be a walking meditation. Then you will feel a gentle background of peace that cannot be disturbed and always returned to no matter what is happening.

It is interesting that, at death, pure calm arises for many when they give up resistance and expectation. There is nothing to be achieved, there is nothing that can be done.

It is during the acceptance phase of death, of which Elizabeth Kubler Ross spoke in her many near-death studies, that this arises.(17) It is your natural state without the ego.

This state is cultivated by adopting right belief, right practice and right action. It is the state you will reach when you *awaken*.

How can I stop my mind from judging in the midst of daily living and interaction?

The ego's task is to judge and define and separate everything. The ego judges by going back to the past and comparing what is happening now to an expectation from the past. If it is not met the ego erupts.

Its access to data to make that judgment, however, is based solely on its own input which is itself restricted. Its nature is the negative, destruction, decay – the opposite of growth and creativity. Therefore, it can only observe the negative, so all of its strategies for dealing with life are negative. It says to you, "I will protect you in the future." Its method of protection is constructed, however, from negative input from the past and invariably creates the very thing it seeks to avoid.

If you are trapped in a cycle of choosing the wrong men, the ego will have modeled someone earlier in your life who did not value the feminine, did not understand it, and treated you inappropriately. The ego uses that model to choose men for you. Whilst it does not bring the relationship you desire, it is the only model the ego has to use. It cannot access the positive of the earlier model, only its negative. Its judging mechanism is flawed from the beginning.

To avoid having the present reality removed from you, you will need to separate your voice from that of the ego. If you hear its comments, or even feel a slight negative reaction to something that has occurred, use it to enhance your awareness. Watch the comments as they arise and allow them to pass by. This is a great training exercise in awareness, but despite the good intentions of some teachings, it will not permanently remove the judgments.

The only permanent solution is to reach the truth and bring the peace back into everyday living. Only then will you experience the benefit of truly being *awake*. A mind that is at peace, with no judgment at all.

Chapter 3

THE PRACTICES:

REACHING THE DIVINE

What is grace? You keep referring to it. Why is it important? How do we find it?

Grace is the cumulative result of karma. It is divine energy received at the right moment to open an understanding and give an experience that will lead to the truth.

To receive it, you must surrender what you think you know and move away from believing the ego's interpretation of the world.

At some point you will be touched by the divine in a way which is not describable with words. It is experienced in this life only and it will pass away as you return your focus to the current reality. You will have a moment of it, then it will pass but leave with you an indelible sense of the truth.

Jesus said:

> *And I will ask the Father, and he will give you another*
> *advocate to help you and be with you forever — the*
> *Spirit of truth. The world cannot accept him, because*
> *it neither sees him nor knows him. But you know him,*
> *for he lives with you and will be [a] in you.*(7)

What Jesus refers to is grace. In that experience you know that you have experienced something different and not of this universe. Again, do not chase this experience. It is merely the road to the destination. Move to the destination – that is what you are seeking to do.

The Buddha explained that his many lives had accumulated karma, his word for grace, which allowed him with clear intent and clear mind to find the truth. It does not have to take many lives to accumulate grace; if your intent is clear enough, it can happen in this life.

Buddha also spoke of the eightfold path. It was his way of explaining a method of building karma. These comprise right view, right intention, right speech, right action, right livelihood, right effort, right mindfulness, and right concentration.

These actions build the energy, or vibration, of connection with the divine, allowing you to reach it during the deep trance of meditation or sometimes in another spontaneous way.

Grace comes after correct preparation. Doing good is not done because it's the right thing to do. Its correct purpose is always to build karma as the right of passage to reach the divine, to *awaken*.

How do we attract karma?

Every action has an equal and opposite reaction. The good things you do attract a higher level of vibration and the bad a lower level. These affect your soul and the energy it can rise to. Enough positive, and your soul moves closer to the divine and in doing so moves away from the influence of the ego. Life becomes simple and quiet. Good things seem to attract to you because of this shift.

As you attract more karma, your ability to open to experiences of the divine is increased, and the more the experiences, the more your certainty rises until you know for yourself what is true. This means taking action, doing things that are in accordance with what the divine is. As you do this, that vibration, or energy, attracts and accumulates to you, bringing more of the same.

The more negative actions you do, the more the ego is convincing in its statements that this belief system is absurd. The further you move away from the divine, the more you become lost in egoic thought patterns and the more that belief in the divine and the truth seems absurd. Logic and ego must be correct. Life becomes hard and more negative things happen as you fall further into the destruction that the ego represents.

As you focus more on taking control of your thoughts and undertaking right actions you will want to be around those whose energy levels are at the same level of consciousness as yours. You will move into a neighborhood where people are more aware. The more you move into rapport with them at this consciousness level, the more karma of a similar nature you will attract. Have you ever noticed how the rich get richer and the poor get poorer. This is how that principle applies. It is not luck or random coincidence; it is karma at its more obvious.

Unfortunately, unless you awaken, the negative karma will continue to be drawn to you. Once caught in the cycle, more and more problems seem to arise. Your car breaks down, you forget to pay the registration, you lose your license because of unpaid speeding fines. These problems are all inspired by the ego. By using its filtering, it ensures you miss important information. The vibration and culture you now inhabit ensure you become unaware. The more unaware you become, the more negative karma you attract as you generate more negative energy.

Certain suburbs in all cities are examples of this principle at work. They have high levels of crime, unemployment and social problems.

You may then take drugs to assist you to cope with the increasing levels of emotional pain and to distance yourself from a reality you cannot bear. The further you sink into this unreality, the further you are from the divine. If you pass to another life now, your birth will reflect the level of karma you take with you.

As you increase your negative karma, so too your level of delusion increases. It then becomes very easy to be lost in the delusion and focus on what appears real.

By moving to understand the teachings by carrying out the practices, the more you will be in connection with the divine. As you do so, right action will naturally follow. No longer bound by the ego you effortlessly take right action, thereby attracting positive karma. This is not the purpose of *awakening*. It is merely a byproduct.

Karma is only required as a bridge to the divine. This is your natural state.

What does the heart and love have to do with *awakening*?

Your heart is vital to *awakening*. It is the seat of your soul and connection to the divine. The heart energy center of your body connects to your divine consciousness and allows you to create balance between the divine in you and the ego. It is an essential element in becoming the perfect vessel to receive grace.

Your body is made of energy. Each center serves a purpose.

Your heart allows you to feel the beauty and serenity around you. It is the instrument of the *awakened* through which to sense things beyond the normal senses. There are nine dimensions of the senses. We can only experience five. The others are:

- Beyond death
- The divine
- The future
- The past.

Following the practices, these can be sensed using your consciousness. Once again let me caution you. These will not bring you the truth. Only direct experience will. These are stepping stones on the path to the divine. Do not lose yourself on the finger pointing to the stars.

The experience of past lives merely serves to confirm that you are immortal. Do not become focused on speaking with those who have passed or on your past lives or future ones. The time to *awaken* is always now.

The heart is the part of the body that connects best with these senses. Through connection to your heart, you will find it easier to connect to the altered states. Directing your consciousness and awareness to your heart is essential.

Buddha said, "The way is not in the sky, the way is in the heart."(1) And Jesus said, "Blessed are the pure in heart, for they will see God."(7) Both were referring to the connection between your heart and freeing the mind as being essential to experiencing the divine. Once you have experienced the truth, the natural state of who you are arises from your heart.

The heart can be best opened through meditation and correct breathing. It then becomes the source of freeing yourself.

What does the divine want us to do?

There is no expectation from the divine to do anything. It has infinite patience as to what has to be done, as it has had always. This does not grant an excuse to do nothing however. That choice is ego inspired and commits us to further karma.

The divine only wants us to realize the truth. It does not create famines or disasters or influence the direction of events. It does not punish and is not in any way vengeful or negative. These notions come from our ego in its delusion. The divine just waits for us to experience what is real. That the ego is the source of all suffering and in separating from the divine we became lost in creations caused by this separation. That there is a way home again and that is *awakening* to the truth.

Our only real direction is to move to the truth as an experience. From that place, right action occurs, negative karma ceases and the vibration of the universe alters for everyone that does.

Eventually the universe will cease, as its purpose to separate from the divine will cease.

The divine is always sending you messages to guide you to *awaken*. These come through someone whom you meet, through songs, through movies. The message is always the same, *awaken*. There are messages and coincidences around you all the time. But the ego will use its selective filtering to keep you busy, to keep you unbalanced and to keep you away from the peace where the message will become clear. The more you find peace, the more you will connect to the divine.

The more you allow events or people to upset you, the more you move into delusion. Consider when an event happens, and what has happened is not what you had anticipated, or when your lover responds in a way that you did not expect. Suddenly the ego is in full flight: you raise your voice, frustration erupts. The ego's plan has been upset; a rule has been breached about how others should act. This is a primary ego function. It ensures you do not rest in peace.

You will truly be *awake* when what occurs around you does not cause you to react.

The divine has no expectations of you. You are part of it. It will not force you to do anything. It is passive in this respect.

How does the ego filter?

The ego filters all the time. It is constantly judging everything. It listens to what someone says and judges it. There is no objectivity. The opinion is compared to the ego's database of beliefs and then altered to suit its beliefs. All such beliefs are part of both the collective and the personal ego.

Ever been with a friend when someone says something to them, they take offence at it and you wonder why? You did not hear the same thing as they did. That is egoic filtering.

Some people have lives full of drama. They listen through their ego and there are always problems. They misinterpret who is really their friend and allow themselves to be used. They then wonder why the world is so mean to them. Others interpret the world as a dangerous place, while some see people as their competitors and project the hate they feel onto them. This occurs in bashings, stealing, break-ins and other crimes. The ego is consumed with rage and projects it onto others; it feels if it can hurt another its own pain will stop.

This is of course false. Their own pain now increases as they do more bad things, and the ego criticizes them for what they have done. There is always inside us a level of awareness of right action even if the ego is dominant.

At a more basic level, knowledge does not win out. The ego will use your pain. You know that eating too much chocolate is bad for you. This is knowledge. You also know that if it's in the fridge you will eat too much of it. The emotional pull the ego exerts overrides your intelligence and your intellect.

Smokers know this well. They are totally conscious that smoking may harm them, but they continue to smoke because the ego rewards them emotionally with time out and connection to themselves in the ego's limited way – rewards offered by the ego to filter out the knowledge that this will likely kill them.

At a collective level, the ego binds delusion together as a national thought system, as in Nazi Germany and Communist Russia. It also occurs when an economy is booming: the collective delusion leads to greed on a massive scale.

It occurs regarding environmental damage where the result is predictable but nations fail to act. It occurs where wars break out or genocide occurs and nations fail to act. They stand by and watch the collective ego take hold.

The ego can also use intellect and intelligence to blind you. It can lose you in intellectual argument about moral or scientific truths, which merely serves to distract you from experience of the divine. An experience it tells you cannot be trusted. Your own intellect will fool you too and tell you esoteric experiences are not real.

It can be difficult to grasp that all thought originates in the ego.

The absurdity of these arguments shows the subtlety of the ego. The ego argues that you require proof. But all proof originates in experience. You must use your senses to observe proof. Intellect stops at the moment of singularity where all known laws cease. Beyond that point only experience is real.

However, the ego says that an internal experience can be faked but an external one cannot. Hypnotism shows that external experiences can be altered. Quantum physics shows that the view of the subatomic world alters with whoever is viewing it. (18)

This is the ego's great lie. What you view with your eyes is not real. All matter is energy. All energy originates from the singularity. The singularity is currently inexplicable by physics.

It is explicable in experience though. The ego will deny this and say, "Rely on your mind." This will only lead to delusion. Using the mind as a tool to find the divine is its correct application.

To experience the truth means to emerge from delusion.

Don't other spiritual practices such as chanting, fortune telling, drumming, sweat lodges all seek bliss? Don't they lead to enlightenment?

There is only one path, one way and one truth. It can be very easy when seeking a spiritual *awakening* to get lost on the road. These side roads are all delusions erected by the ego. They are attempting to create grace or a moment of enlightenment, which is what bliss is. But they don't break through and have it last as wisdom. You may experience bliss during chanting as your mind moves to another state. You may experience it during meditation but, like all things, it is transitory. It does not last. The only stable state is that which comes from the divine. In its purest form it is love, but a love that we do not experience here and only at times briefly glimpse.

These other practices can provide those moments, but they can also be used by the ego as an addictive drug. Many are temporarily lost on the road to seeking those experiences and far more emotive ones in their search to *awaken*.

Awakening is about following right thought, based in a belief that acknowledges your true state as immortal, never to be harmed, and then right action in your day-to-day interactions, leading to the only proven way to directly know for yourself the divine and lastly to separation from the ego. You cannot, however, force yourself to think in the correct way or perform the right action. This attempt will fail because the autopilot of the ego will cut back in and you will be lost in negative patterns of behavior again.

The ego can ensure it is easy to be lost in all forms of religion. All thought originates from the ego, but this can be difficult to see initially. All thought is created by the ego to hide what is obvious when you are still and quiet and not thinking.

Without correct interpretation of the ancient teachings, the true meaning becomes obscured and will lead you to spend many years lost in the ego's logic.

What happens when I practice getting closer to the divine?

Through pure concentration during meditation and carrying out the practices you will move to higher levels of direct experience and you will notice there is less drama in your life. It becomes quieter, more focused and peaceful.

The journey has stages and each stage must be passed before the next will occur for you. They cannot be rushed. They must each be experienced by you. Be assured that the divine is there with you.

There will be many signposts along the way that cannot be written off as chance. They become noticeable and statistically too frequent to ignore.

Money no longer is a concern, bills are paid on time, speeding fines are a thing of the past. New opportunities open for you. In the different vibration in which you now live, your positive karma attracts different people to you. You move in different circles from before. Karmically, you attract those who share the same journey as you and you learn from them and give learning to them. Life now has purpose.

You move through life, secure in the knowledge that this is one small moment in an eternity of living. As Lao Tzu reflected:

> *Before enlightenment, chopping wood carrying water, after enlightenment, chopping wood carrying water.*(4)

Nothing has changed, but everything has changed.

What other spiritual practices should I follow if I want the truth?

Many spiritual practices are soundly based in reaching the truth. Like anything, though, the ego can use them. Many ascetic practices, religions and belief systems are based in the ego. Buddha saw this and found a middle way, specifically requesting his followers not to make a religion from his teachings.

They of course did out of fear of not being able to find their own way.

Being harsh on yourself is a large part of the ego's hold over you. It criticizes and sets you up to fail. It will use past pain to compel you to do something, then bitterly criticize you afterwards for being weak or bad for having given in to the impulse to do it. This includes any time things don't work out for you, or you make a mistake, eat chocolate, fail to exercise or any other things that the ego can find fault with.

You may use the power of your will or adhere to values to ensure you behave in a certain way. This will not attract good karma, nor will it work in the long term, because the ego will ensure you go back to your old way of doing it. Karma comes from being *awake*. From that state you will attract good karma because that is in connection with the divine. It is the closeness of the connection that brings it. It is not wishful thinking. That is the ego. The ego is always wishing for something and is focused on one person, itself.

You cannot place the cart before the horse. You cannot attract good karma when you do a right action because it is the right thing to do. You can only attract good karma after connection with the divine because doing right action from that place is in alignment with who you are.

That's why Jesus told the parable of the farmer planting his seed in Mark 4:3-9.(7) The seed only took root in the well-prepared soil. He meant that you must prepare well your awareness and consciousness for the connection to occur. Without preparation, your consciousness cannot pierce the veil of the ego.

Correct meditation practice is necessary. The intent during meditation must be to commune with the divine not to sit in a search for peace or exotic experience in deep trance. There are correct methods of reaching the divine during meditation and Rapid Induction Meditation is designed to bring you quickly to that place.

Harshness in order to reach the truth is also not necessary and is detrimental.

Overeating or using alcohol as a means of changing your state and how you feel is not necessary and weakens the connection to your soul. To be clear in your body enhances your vibration and your energy and allows you to reach the altered levels of consciousness more easily.

Eating a reduced amount, even fasting on some days, will enhance the "lightness" of your body. Fasting too much will serve the ego not the divine. The need to have a drink to relax is part of the ego's way of diverting you from the "feeling" of your true essence. Coffee too, or anything that alters the "clear" state of your physical body, will not assist.

Extremes in any of these habits will result in your quest falling further into delusion and being caught up in the ego's desire to have more.

A homeless person's ego is seeking more. It tells them that they don't need to be part of society, that it is they who are the smart ones not caught up in the rat race. They have the real freedom. The ego has succeeded in achieving the impossible. By having them give up everything, it has given them more freedom.

That is the ego's insane thought system.

Some seek the truth experience through drugs. This is ego inspired. Whilst those who follow this road may experience altered states of reality, they are not altered states of consciousness that lead to the truth. They are diversions away from it.

The drug culture is ego inspired and keeps you trapped in a false reality. It says you can handle the drug, but the truth is the drug has you. Drug taking is based in the ego.

Some may say this is taking all the joy out of life, that drugs are enjoyable in moderation. But look around. Every day beauty and joy is all around you. In the garden, watching the ocean, in your children's eyes, in that flower that has just bloomed, in a beautiful song or a magnificent landscape. The feeling is clear, pure, because it relates to your soul, to your home, where there is nothing but peace. The vibration level is stillness.

This stillness is naturally yours when you *awaken*.

Drugs do not bring joy. This journey does.

You can enhance your connection with the divine when you walk through a forest, watch waves crash, stand on a mountain looking over a valley, listen to music that evokes the peace within you. Anywhere you can sense the creative force, it is the divine. This will bring recollection to the heart. Through this, you will remember.

These experiences will remind you of what the divine is, but it is still not the experience you must have.

Keep your body clean through balance in exercise, food intake and sleep, and no drugs. It really is the temple of your soul.

You will move much closer to experiencing the truth.

Can you explain this way to the truth simply to me?

To release from the ego is a journey, not a moment. However, this is your ultimate purpose. This is certain.

Step one is to wish to reach the truth. To truly want to know it. You must be at the point in your karma where this becomes more important than any other task.

Step two involves finding the patterns that come from this life and have been passed down by your family, events in your life or the culture you grew up in. You have adopted these through modeling.

In step three, you resolve these so that you are free of the pain and therefore of the ego's hold over you. The more pain you hold, the greater the ego's ability to use it to control your emotions.

Now seek an experience of the truth, the reality of the place that is your home and where you can be clear that your soul is immortal. That can only come via grace or in meditation. If you attempt this step, as many do, before you have cleared this karma, you will not reach the truth. To pass through the veil that holds this experience, you must be clear in body, mind and spirit. You must have developed what is termed by the Buddhists "the eye of contemplation". In the Hindu religion it is called "the third eye", which means using your internal sight of focus inwardly to await the divine.

Once you have seen the truth you will have a clarity of purpose. You will live in this universe but exist in another. You will do what you need to do but have a greater purpose. You will know of past and future lives and connections with all those around you and the greater connectedness of yourself with all others. Compassion for the unaware is a natural result of this step.

The truth is that you are divine. You are creative, you are at peace and you are in tune with the Yang, or positive, in the universe. When you rest in the positive, life is a joy because you are in alignment with the silence, the space between time. The only moment is now and that's what you are. Living in the moment feels nothing but pure joy because there are no concerns, nothing is a threat and there can be no fear. That is what the truth is.

That is what every spiritual master has said in various forms and ways.

With this experienced and resting in the truth, you must be clear of negative karma. You must do this by deed and action. The time this takes is up to you. It can take one lifetime or many. What occurs really is your perception of how long it takes extends as all time really occurs now.

Step one is the release of the patterns that bind you to a false ego image of yourself and hold you to actions that do not bring you closer to the divine – actions which are not in accordance with its nature. Step one is a journey that is best taken with others. This takes enormous courage. It is far easier to see the ego in others than in yourself. It can also be completed with a trusted person. Rarely is it done singly.

Lack of progress in this step is never the divine not accepting us, it is always us undertaking thought or action that is not in accord with what the divine is. It is our ego delusion that we are different from the divine and that we need acceptance. This is what the ego believes. We must cease these actions and thoughts to stop being the ego and become our true nature.

There are modes or therapies that can shift you from an unawakened state to an altered one where the ego can be put aside for that moment. Modalities such as Neuro-Linguistic Programming (NLP), hypnotism, Cognitive Behavior Therapy (CBT), Emotional Transformation Therapy (ETT) and *Rational Emotive Behavior Therapy* (REBT) all create different states in which the ego is put aside for a moment, a month, or a year. But these will not give you access to the truth. These are roads that can lead there. These modalities do not create permanent change. The ego will return in another form, problem or issue.

Awareness of the creation of a pattern clearly seen is the best solution to step one. When an event occurred when you were a child, the ego decided that it meant something. The story it told about the event was only one interpretation of the event, but because it was the ego's version, the meaning was negative. You must undo this version through awareness of the delusion. In seeing the reality, the behavoural pattern it created collapses. You will then be free to choose to view this event in a different way.

Step two is a personal journey that a master can guide you on but none can do for you or accompany you on. This is the inward journey to experience the truth. You will not find the divine in an outer experience, only signposts pointing to it, no master can give it to you, nor any amount of joy or belief in positive mantras, or the beauty of the birth of a child. You may certainly observe the divine in a beautiful sunset or the energy of a forest, but this is still not a personal experience of the divine. This inner journey is one of concentration and meditation. This takes enormous focus. As Buddha said:

> No one saves us but ourselves. No one can and no one may. You yourselves must walk the path.(1)

Lao Tzu said:

> Tao exists in one's own true self.
> It cannot be found outside of one's true nature.
> Hence, there is no need to leave the house to take [a] journey in order to know the world.
> There is no need to look outside of the window to see the nature of Tao.
> The further one departs from Tao, the less one will be able to know.(4)

He says here that the knowledge of Tao is not enough, you must experience it for yourself. These are key words to show you the way. The further you depart from these, the less you will understand.

This journey is the same as Buddha's on the night of his enlightenment. The first part of the journey is to face the ego's delusions and pierce the veil of its deception. The second part is to become clear on past lives. The third and final part is to experience the interconnectedness of all life and the grand tapestry of our souls.

During stage two meditation you will feel the pull of the ego and be distracted. You will find it difficult to focus without thoughts constantly pulling you away from silence. Bring your attention inward and ask your quiet mind what events, past or present, this distraction relates to. What events in life are still karmically unresolved inside yourself? What do you need to forgive yourself or others for? What things have you done that you still want to do? What events has your ego told you a lie about?

This process became the distorted Christian practice of Confession. Its real purpose was to undertake this questioning and personal accounting and move to be in alignment with the divine nature.

Once you have identified them with your quiet mind during meditation, let them go. Release them from yourself. You cannot join to the divine without silence inside and purity in your heart. Purity comes from forgiving. It comes from right decisions and right actions. It comes from you believing you are ready, and it comes from you combining right action with right thought and letting go of attachment to deeds you have done or making amends internally for deeds others hold you responsible for. This is why the Buddha developed the eightfold path: to set out a process of joining with the divine, which is ultimately joining with yourself.

Step three must be taken only in the service of all others. This is the final portion of the journey to find your true purpose, which is aligned to the greater purpose of *awakening* all. It will not be a goal of the ego. It is the journey of the accomplished. This will come from joining your heart and your quiet mind.

The Tao expresses it thus:

> *In pursuing Tao, one is enlightened with the true nature and thus diminishes daily one's worldly desires. The continuous depletion of one's desires persists until one acts accordingly to the natural Way.*(4)

To reduce your attachments or desires, Rapid Induction Meditation (RIM) is useful. RIM is a method of reaching deep states of connection quickly. This is how you can use it.

Picture, as you close your eyes, going down a set of escalators. As you descend, count down from 10 to 1, then repeat 4 times, going deeper each time. As you reach the bottom of the escalator, imagine stepping into white light. Draw to you the feeling of the divine and place yourself into the same state as the divine – clear, feeling blessed, fully conscious. Repeat the mantra "Deeper, deeper" and continue to repeat it as you feel yourself going further into a different plane. You will feel a flood of connection occur and a feeling of profound peace.

Alternatively, place your hand in front of your face, palm towards you. Begin to move the palm towards your nose saying to yourself "deeper". Allow yourself to move into a trance state and to sink more deeply into the trance, tell yourself that when it reaches your nose you will be in a deep trance.

Then concentrate your focus to the point between your eyes. You will begin to see images. Keep focused on them. Do not at this point allow your focus to drift. Keep intense presence and awareness on the images and lights you can see. Feel a connection to those images and ignore any distractions which may arise. Stay focused and true to your purpose and you will experience intuition from the divine source of all consciousness. You will become clear on your connection and what you need to do in your life to express it. Stay in it until you feel there is no more you need to know.

Initially you can focus on direct experience of other lives to provide proof to yourself. Later it may be about what you need to do in your life – perhaps clarity on the patterns that keep you deluded by the ego and from where those patterns originated. For each person the experience will be unique but with one common theme: clear consciousness that is calm and at peace that you can bring into each day.

This where you will have direct experience so you truly "know" the truth yourself not because someone has told you about it.

An instructor in RIM can assist you to master this method. If you require one, please refer to the website: www.awakenbook.com.

Every day you spend in this meditation will bring you closer to knowledge of the divine through experience.

Every lie the ego told you about each event that created each pattern is what creates each desire. You must rid yourself of every pattern. Each of these steps must be experienced to fully comprehend their real meaning. No words can convey the actuality of having taken this step.

The ego would have you believe this journey is difficult and cannot be achieved. It wants you to believe that you are powerless.

However, the truth is, when we band together, we can stop tyrants, end wars, eradicate starvation, create a heaven on earth. These are not the goal though. They will initially be the result. These are the ways of attracting the correct karma, which will lead to changing the world.

The ego will distract you and use up time, which is its creation. In the divine there is no time, there is only the moment. In the ego there is only the past and the future, never the moment.

It will speak of how frustrating this process is. It will tell you it is fruitless and you have better things to do, other priorities. These are all delusion. This is your ultimate journey and no other exists.

Begin it now and you will find your way home.

How do I take the first step and remove the patterns?

Awareness and consciousness dispel the delusion.

Initially you must experience clearly that each life attaches to the collective ego as it grows, but also comes with its own unique karma when born.

You only need to look at a child to observe and confirm that each comes with an innate personality and traits. Some are fiery and like to push back and resist authority, whilst others are more pleasing and seek to obey. These patterns will accentuate and grow in this life. Events will occur that are in accordance with those patterns. The patterns, which are karmic in nature, draw events that confirm what the ego believes.

As an event arises, it will overlay a similar event from the past and, using a pattern, will have you react in the same way.

If you were treated without respect when you were little, an unspoken and unexpressed rage will slowly build. In adulthood, one small incident of being treated without respect will cause the rage to explode. This is the ego's plan to protect you. Indeed, it does, but only with regard to the emotion of respect; it will not see the damage done to relationships, to your self-esteem and to other people's opinions of you. The ego will ignore all these. Also, you will notice the pattern takes effect before conscious thought can prevent it.

That is why it is necessary to bring these patterns of reaction into the light of awareness. The ego tells you that they are just you, that's how you behave, thereby keeping the patterns in the dark.

Once you can recognise a pattern, it comes into consciousness and its power to control you is lessened. It is like slowly peeling back an onion. The more layers you peel, the closer you come to the core.

Consider your past. What patterns were created when you were younger? What event formed those patterns and what meaning did you put on that event? Meditating on these questions can reveal the answers to you. In this awareness, the patterns collapse.

A hard-working man owned a small manufacturing business. With a wife and two children and seven employees, he had many responsibilities. He was always busy and noticeably stressed. Things were never done to his satisfaction, so he had to do most things himself, including invoicing, pricing of jobs, supervising assembly and checking installations. Even though he had enough money to employ better people to do these things, he did not. Why?

An egoic pattern. Whilst his intellect told him he should hire better people, his ego argued that he couldn't afford it, despite the financial evidence to the contrary. The ego's filter ensured he could not see this, so he remained busy and not available to his family.

This is the power of patterns.

The ego uses patterns to control your responses to life's events. If you do not break the patterns, you have no freedom. This is why it is the first step to *awakening*.

How does the ego keep us from seeing the truth?

The ego loves distraction. It will create drama in your life – mostly around what should happen to it. It has firm demands about what should happen. How, when and why. If those rules are broken by an event or a person it will react with anger.

The ego's reaction is designed to generate negative energy, which it thrives on because that's what it is. This filtering is perfect for generating negative energy because it has so many expectations and rules that it is inevitable they will be broken and anger in all its forms will be generated.

It is the Yin of the Tao and it can only exist with that energy being created in everything, including you. Its forces of destruction can be observed in nature as everything either grows or dies, as does your body. There is only one thing in this universe that this does not apply to. Your consciousness. It is part of the divine and never dies.

The ego makes annoyance its primary tool. Consider in one day how many things occur that annoy you. If you are aware, you will notice that there are hundreds. Annoyance is another form of anger, itself the primary form of destructive energy described in the Tao. Awareness is the antidote to this affliction that takes away the peace of who you really are.

Initially, as a practice move into a state of decision that you will accept everything as it happens. Once that practice becomes established, you will find you connect more to your heart and, through it, experience the peace that you seek.

The ego will always have you focus on some form of distraction. By its nature the universe is meaningless. So you must focus on something to give it meaning as the ego cannot let you see that it has no meaning. Not unless it can bring you to hopelessness, then it may convince you to kill yourself to end the pain.

For most personal egos, though, lack of meaning is avoided. The ego needs us to have something to spend our time doing. Work occupies many. Food, a cause of some type, lack of fitness, laziness or another behavior it can criticize you for, glory or power, partying, over-parenting, serving others at cost to ourselves and many other forms of behavior that become repetitive patterns. These are focused on by the ego to ensure your time is used up in illusion rather than questioning the reality of the world you live in.

The movie, *The Matrix*, is a metaphor for this concept.(12) It demonstrates the basic illusion that the ego holds in front of us. It appears real until the signal is disrupted and Neo, the "chosen one" of the movie, experiences the "truth". That it is all a scheme for holding humanity in a prison for the mind.

Whilst merely a dramatization of this ancient truth, it still resonates as another message to illustrate the working of the ego. In the final part three of the series, Neo ends up merging with the computer behind the matrix. He is finally home.

The metaphor is true for all of you. You are also the "chosen one" and your journey is to discover the truth which is hidden from you by an apparent reality.

What is the practice during meditation that will help me experience the truth?

In the initial stages of meditation there will be many thoughts. You will hear external sounds. Bring your focus internally and focus on your breathing and what you can see with your eyes closed.

You will notice thoughts and images as they appear, as the ego attempts to keep you focused on daily matters of this world. Keep bringing yourself back to the breath and the colors you can see internally as points of focus.

Thoughts will arrive and so will stories. You will find yourself sucked into them as the ego drags you down the path with them. Keep your awareness high and bring yourself back to the breathing and what you see. Keep doing this. Use the power of your concentration.

It may take over an hour or more. Make sure you allow yourself enough time. Once you have moved beyond the normal passing of thoughts and images, you will reach the first stage of peace. Here, you must use internal sight, often called the eye of contemplation, meaning to use your internal vision to experience the divine and hear its message clearly.

Move your state to one of the higher emotions, love for all sentient beings, joy or compassion, and feel the divine move to you. You will literally feel its energy around you. Now focus internally on what you see, and feel yourself pierce the veil of delusion. The light of the divine will be with you as you feel yourself floating in a clear field of consciousness. The voice that now speaks is not that of your ego.

Soon your focus will cause an *awakening* and connection with the divine. You will experience a different voice. A calmer, clearer voice. Seek the truth on your many lives and experiences. See clearly how they all interconnect, how each one leads to another set of experiences that made you grow and is leading you through karma to one outcome. Ask for clarity on the interconnectedness of all life. Experience it as being real, not just a belief.

Keep returning your interior sight to a point of focus and your mind to your breathing. When you drift off, bring your focus back.

Seek direction on what you need to do to live your purpose in this life. Do not be afraid if it suggests something outside of what you expect. Question more on what you need to carry out the task. You will know in your heart if this is true and not your ego speaking as it will have a tone and experience very different from the ego voice you are used to hearing.

To experience this, approach it from a place of patience, without the need of the ego to reach some goal. Be patient, be prepared, keep your awareness high and there will be a moment when it will all change and you will know you have reached communion with the divine.

Being in the moment is a great practice; however, it also is just one step towards the truth of the divine experience you must have. Having had that experience, you do not need to struggle to remain in the present. Practicing remaining in the present is difficult, as many have found, if you have not first been freed from the constraints of the ego. Once freed from its shackles, that practice, as are all others, is in alignment with who you are.

The first place to focus is on having the actual experience, then remaining in the present and acting with compassion will be natural results of this.

Ask and listen. Then you will know it to be true. Then you will *awaken*.

If the ego wants to keep us here and it lives through us, why doesn't it create a perfect world? A heaven on earth?

The ego is not able to create heaven on earth as you put it. It can only create using the knowledge that it possesses. It has no access to the positives of this universe.

Your personal ego collects on a physical level all your negative experiences. It stores them in one part of your mind and body. This part has no access to positive experience. On a global scale it does the same, being the holder of all negative experiences. Therefore it cannot conceive of a heaven on earth. It will use false positives in its plan but ultimately a negative must result from what it does. That is all it knows. The ego thought patterns are the same in all of us. They are based on separation. The ego is in all of us; we were connected to it when we arrived in this universe.

The connection to the divine is also available to all of us but not within the framework of this universe. We must change consciousness to be able to access it.

Then the ego is evil?

Evil is a relative term based on the duality of this universe. The ego is not evil in the sense that a child is not evil when it drops a flower pot to see what happens and it falls on another child's head. It has no intent to be evil. It merely does what is its nature to do.

The ego expresses the negative of this universe as created by us in the separation. It performs that task well. The ego has no intention to do you harm, but in its madness, in its unreality, it believes that it is acting in your best interests even if it kills you.

It is like the story of the computer that becomes self aware. It quickly reaches the conclusion that to protect people it should kill them all because they are the biggest threat to themselves, and that consciousness is better to exist in a machine.

The ego speaks protection to you but delivers pain and misery. An event, a moment, a conversation is not just that. The ego will distort and make it something else.

Seeing the ego as evil is not a correct frame through which to view its nature. You are not fighting the ego, merely recognizing it for what it is and therefore denying it any influence.

What do I need to do to experience the truth?

No one can explain it to you, nor can you intellectualize it. You cannot understand it. You can read all the Christian, Buddhist, Hindu and Muslim texts and you will still not have it. It must be experienced to know what it is.

All ancient religious texts point to this as a means of reaching the truth. Meditation is one path to reach it. High levels of pain experienced in your life may cause the ego to temporarily cease and you may be blessed with great insight. A decision to give up all things in your life of form may cause it. Once it has, though, the ego will still use the experience to blind you by making you focus on the experience rather than letting go of the ego. The experience is not what you seek.

Accumulating experience in dealing with people's problems can provide insight if it is approached not from an intellectual point of view but from a spiritual one. Counseling or psychology can be useful to point you in the direction of awareness but it doesn't *awaken* you. It provides no experience of the divine, which is necessary to *awaken*.

Studying the ancient texts and books on the journey will assist in pointing you in the right direction and may give you a degree in religious studies, but it will not give you the truth.

All texts regardless of their origin – Tao, Zen, Christian, Muslim, Buddhist – point to the Christ experience, the receiving of grace and the eventual prayer or meditation that is necessary to reach the truth and *awaken*.

You actually need nothing, but given the laws of the ego you will need a method and techniques to *awaken*. At times the ego will fool you. You will believe yourself to be there, only to find it is another mirage set up by the ego. Do not be disheartened. Nurture your resolve to push through. Harness the power of concentration to hold fast to your quest.

Concentration is awareness focused on staying *awake*, which means not allowing yourself during meditation or when you are going about your daily tasks to enter into delusion. In meditation it is experienced as focus on what is happening now. The same is true with your eyes open.

By practicing inward sight during meditation, it translates to an increased sense of calm when you are not meditating. You bring the divine with you into this world and carry that sense of deep insight into everything you do and see. You are not deluded by others' behaviors. You will see those behaviors as merely a lack of understanding caused by illusion.

You will experience seeing others as connected to you and not separate, and through this experience true compassion arises.

A beautiful practice during daily talks is not to attribute meaning to anything that is said or done. This method will help you with this practice. "Feel" the presence and awareness inside yourself, but do not mentally project or construct that you have presence. However, if you pull your focus inwards, you can feel your own life force. Once you become aware of your inner presence, use it to look outwards at the world and its events. Become passive and the watcher of what occurs. As you become the watcher, make decisions and speak from that place so you do not allow the ego to place meaning on anything. This practice will train your mind to let go of what you think you know and experience what really happens.

The focus and strength to carry out these practices comes from karma, meaning undertaking right action. Build enough of it and you will allow yourself to find what you seek. As you perform more right action, you move more into alignment with the divine. It is like watching a movie. You can enjoy what happens but at the end you can leave without it being your life. There is a sense that you are connected to another world whilst being in this one. You can laugh more and not take yourself and others so seriously.

I can't seem to focus during meditation. Why?

It can be a strange experience for the mind to grasp that the physical world is a delusion. The mind is designed to experience the world and it is the ego's main tool to prove that what you see is real. The truth is that all sight is merely light vibrations stimulating atoms and registering in your brain as electrical signals. Hearing is merely your ear drum vibrating to sound waves vibrating atoms in the air. All touch is atoms speeding up or slowing down.

What we all experience is caused by atomic reactions all around us. It is a great tapestry of atomic phenomena painted on a quantum canvas. One that appears real to all of us, but is not.

This spiritual truth has been evident since the universe has been in existence. The Mayans knew it, the Babylonians as early as the 11th century BC in the Enûma Eliš(19), Egyptians in their creation myths, Indians in the Hindu religion and the Chinese in the Tao.

Science knows it. Therefore, is it so difficult to grasp that what you see with your eyes is energy and matter made of miniscule particles that are constantly changing based on our collective agreement as to how they occur?

The latest research shows that particles can exist in two places at once defying the normal laws of physics.(20) Does this not speak to you that all is not what it seems?

This delusion is the effect you feel during meditation. If you pierce through the veil through the power of your consciousness, then it collapses and you will have an experience of connection and clarity with the divine. The collective ego prevents this from occurring because it does not want that connection. Its primary purpose is to prevent it.

In preventing it, it frustrates you. You all know you want a deeper connection. The divine is knowable only within the context of the way this universe exists. You cannot know the divine in this delusion of the ego. So while your senses are flooded with the ego you cannot reach the present moment and experience the divine. You can only do this once outside it. That's what meditation, grace or a spontaneous experience can allow you to do.

Persevere, but do not make a quest out of the result.

You asked about focus. Concentration during meditation can allow you to pass through many stages. This is described well in the Pali, the ancient Buddhist text:

> *Through meditation wisdom is gained;*
> *through lack of meditation wisdom is lost.*(1)

What you seek is deepening of the state of peace to a point where there is no arising of awareness from outside of where your awareness is. Now. Then a spontaneous arising of awareness occurs but this time one you welcome, one that feels like home. One that provides unfiltered insight to the nature of reality and your own life.

You will require patience to experience this. Correct action to build karma, pure desire and pure concentration are required as preparatory work, all unaffected by the ego. Then await grace. You will feel the change – from ego space to divine space. From divine space the three truths can be directly experienced: the truth of many lives, the truth of interconnectedness and the truth of the divine itself.

This is true knowledge and can only be reached with sufficient time and force of consciousness to remain focused and aware. This is the result of patience.

How do I bring the divine into everyday living?

The ego loves the drama involved in everyday living. That's why it uses patterns to recreate it all the time.

Watch any soap on TV and you will see your own life reflected in the never-ending problems and issues that arise. The ego creates them all. It is the sole proprietor of all the negativity you experience in the world. It exists in all of you and gains its energy from what it creates.

Even if we weren't here as an expression of the divine, it would still do so in the interaction between animals, the eat or be eaten reflex you can observe in nature, and in the dying of stars in the cosmos. It is an integral part of the universe and cannot be removed. It can only be seen for what it is. Not real.

To live in the divine each day can be accomplished by existing in a state that is supported by the divine, by bringing out of the direct connection with it the peace of mind that the divine has. To remain with it requires you to fully surrender to it. That can be the experience whilst meditating. Even once you have pierced the veil of the illusion intending to fully surrender, you will be confronted by fear of what you will lose. The ego will still attempt to create emotions that will hold you.

Grace plays a part here. Jesus spoke of it this way:

> *Behold, I stand at the door and knock. If anyone hears my voice and opens the door, I will come in to him and eat with him, and he with me.*(7)

He was of course not speaking literally. The meaning he was conveying was to seek the intervention of grace to enter into that place. Grace will come to you if the preparation is done. To get there you must emanate the same level of peace as the divine. Then you will experience the truth.

Jesus also spoke of the preparation that is necessary:

> *Enter by the narrow gate. For the gate is wide and the way is easy that leads to destruction, and those who enter by it are many. For the gate is narrow and the way is hard that leads to life, and those who find it are few.*(7)

Without preparation you will not see it. Once you have prepared, bringing it into your day will be natural.

Buddha also spoke of the preparation and resolve that enabled him to reach *awakening*.

What happens after death?

If you refer to the stages in between lives, then the *Tibetan Book of the Dead* describes in detail the process through which the soul passes from one life to the next.(21) A recent and more popular edition of this work is a book titled *The Tibetan Book of the Living and Dying* by Sogyal Rinpoche, which also describes the process and may be easier to read.(22)

The intent of focus at the time of death can have a large impact on your karma in the next life according to the master, Karma Lingpa, who wrote the first book. If you have *awoken* you can maintain your consciousness during the Bardo, the after death plane, and ensure you remember in the next life where you are from and what you wish to accomplish in this new life.

These books provide a beautiful description of the process. You may also wish to read *Return to Life* by Dr. Jim Tucker, a University of Virginia professor who has studied 2500 cases of children's reincarnation, or listen to him speaking on video or radio.(11)

The continual cycle of death and life is caused by your attachment to the ego and your failure to separate from it and the delusions of the universe that we see and experience. If you seek to leave behind the continual suffering that you experience, then *awakening* is the path for you to follow.

Death is merely part of your natural process in this universe on the path to *awaken*. All is well, as *A Course in Miracles* states.(6) The divine in you, the essence of you moves from one life to the next. This is your consciousness and it can never die. It is the background to the universe and how you experience life. It is life, and what you see before you is the expression of that made manifest.

It is felt not in your mind but through your heart as the sensing organ that allows you to feel. All thought is of the ego. Feeling is the way home.

A more important question to answer is what happens when you live?

Are there different levels in the afterlife? Do we have guides or angels that lead us?

The ego is always seeking to understand. It is always wanting to know intellectually – through the mind. Once you have direct experience, you will know the answers to these questions. The truth will be self-evident. It is not helpful to seek the divine through such mediums.

Seek the direct experience yourself. Angels and guides will not bring *awakening*; whilst they may point you in the right direction, only you can realize this for yourself. Many things will guide you in the correct direction if you are open to them but only you are the source of your own *awakening*. The Holy

Spirit was the term Jesus used for these events or messages that you will experience as you seek the divine.

Nothing else, only you.

You will know through personal experience. Then the answer becomes meaningful.

What is life like after *awakening*?

The ego ceases its dance. External events do not upset you. How can you be upset when you know the truth? It truly is the cessation of suffering, as Buddha said.

You still live in this world, the normal things occur, but your responses to them arise from a place of peace. You have emotions. You love, you cry, you feel but these are now based on peace, not fear.

You are freed from patterns of behavior that run unconsciously and keep you suffering. You are free to experience your consciousness in all its beauty and feel the winds of freedom on your face as you make choices that are taking you to where you should be.

The basis of belief has changed. Now life is eternal, not some distant concept but a truth that is central to your being. If a problem occurs, your response comes not from irritation, but from peace because whatever the problem is, it always works out okay.

You still have possessions, you still need to earn money. You still eat and sleep. You are bound by the laws of the universe. What changes is your response to events. You have no claim or desire for an outcome. Whatever outcome occurs is okay with you. You still have goals and dreams but these are secondary to the peace.

You know clearly when the ego is speaking to you. You are not swept up in a thought that leads to an action that you didn't want to occur. The ego never unbalances you again. The perspective is clear. There is no fear.

Your responses are based in peace, love and balance. You know that you must participate in the divine purpose to free others and that becomes your sole purpose in life. You still do the daily things but your life is about others around you. Not in a self-serving way but to free them from bondage to the ego.

You are not concerned with their lifestyles or living situations but how they can *awaken*.

Have you experienced *awakening*?

Yes.

Why are we here?

By its nature, the divine is creative. The moment it had the impulse to create, an energy was brought into existence. That energy is behind evolution and the creative force observed in the universe. You are part of that energy, one expression of that force. The divine moves within that to guide you home again.

The Buddha said:

> *Those who have failed to work toward the truth have missed the purpose of living.*(1)

The moment the energy separated, the awareness that is our consciousness also felt the separation, and to substitute for what it perceived was lost, the ego was formed. This is the original Biblical story of creation. In separation our consciousness moved into delusion.

Now your consciousness is destined to come home, but the more you believe what you see, the greater the delusion caused. The more negative energy (vibration) created, the more the ego expands.

Consider anger. When you are around someone displaying it, you can feel its force. It creates vibration by the force of the voice used, the way the person is breathing, the intensity of cortisol streaming through their veins. Everything is interconnected. Nothing can arise unless dependent on something else. Negative emotions send out vibration, which is energy.

Jesus said:

> You have heard that it was said to the people long ago, "Do not murder, and anyone who murders will be subject to judgment." But I tell you that anyone who is angry with his brother will be subject to judgment.(7)

He was referring to the cause of karma not to God's retribution.

Our journey is to create positive karma and bring all of us home again. Positive karma is another form of energy. It can be felt when someone is kind or sending love. The voice tone changes, pheromones change, the vibration is different. There is an effect in the space–time continuum. This is not theory, it is commonsense. Everything is connected. In chaos theory this is known as the butterfly effect – small changes to a system can invoke chaos.

As explained, this journey outside of this universe has already been completed. Inside is the only place that time exists. Outside, your consciousness is already home.

Knowing this, though, serves no purpose for your *awakening*. That's why Buddha chose not to speak of it. He directed his students to practices that he felt would lead to their own enlightenment. You must choose to come home yourself. The divine would never force you to do so. You have the same creativity in you, and free will to create is yours. Our creation of the ego, though, has kept us away from our true source.

Some may ask, "Why did the divine allow the separation?" That is like asking, "What is the sound of one hand clapping." The divine is creative by nature. Yes, it knew the outcome in the moment the impulse arose, but it is creative. It would never stop its own creation, us, from creating. We have free will. That is why the choice to *awaken* must be ours and can never be forced or withheld by the divine.

No harm can come to you, as will be obvious when you understand the truth.

Is the world changing?

Many are seeking a deeper meaning to life. We cannot ignore that we are far more peaceful now than we have ever been in our history.

The scale of war peaked 70 years ago at the end of World War II. Since then, the ego continues its influence globally with regard to war but its influence has been lessened. We all want more, and many seek answers that intelligence cannot provide. A 2009 Pew survey found that spiritual experiences, defined as a "moment of sudden religious insight or *awakening*", occurs much more frequently now than they did in 1962, 1976 or 1994, when similar studies were done.(23)

You are *awakening*. This book is part of a movement to accelerate it. How quickly is up to you. Will you embrace the message that all religions point to the same truth? Will you then let go enough of what you think you know to fully experience the truth when that letting go feels like giving up something, and that is because you are giving up what the ego doesn't want you to – delusion.

One message that the ego always delivers is, "You will have to give up something." It will say, "Things are good right now, I don't feel the need to grow, I'm okay where I am." This message you believe and it keeps you trapped. Others caught deeper in the ego delusion will say, "This is nonsense, show me the divine. Prove it exists." They will not meditate or prepare themselves for that experience to take place. Their egos want someone else to do it for them.

Jesus said:

> *Do not give what is holy to the dogs; nor cast your pearls before swine, lest they trample them under their feet, and turn and tear you in pieces.(6)*

He was referring to those trapped in their egos, who do not want to see or experience the truth.

As greater awareness arises, the world will become more conscious of what we are doing to the planet:

environmentally abusing resources, ignoring the inherent inequity in the system of haves and have-nots. These issues are all solvable. They can be solved by embracing the truth and seeing that, as the balance changes, we all become one. The change can be expressed as "with what I have, I can assist you". I am not speaking of wealth, but the truth. The physical will then follow.

That becomes the real path of your transformation. It is apparent that that shift of consciousness has already begun. As it moves further, eventually the need for this universe ceases.

If that concept seems unreal to you, consider that the universe came from nothing. Science states that, at our present level of understanding, the Big Bang occurred 15 billion years ago and all matter came from one singularity.(8) That, even to the most skeptical mind, must sound like the divine.

Physicists are believers in observation and want to trust only what they can prove mathematically. However, they cannot answer what happened prior to the Big Bang because, at that point, all laws as they relate to this universe, including space and time, did not operate or exist.

The only proof can be in your own personal experience. You cannot prove it with the mind that created the concept of the universe.

As we move to a new depth of awareness, the world will change. We will begin to look after this ship that we are travelling through space on. We will begin to realize that it cannot support a never-ending stream of people. We will begin to question our system of economic growth based on ever-increasing levels of population growth and consumption. We will see that on a global scale the ego is like a locust. It consumes everything in its path that we allow it to.

Once we *awaken* to these self-evident truths, we will loosen the ego's collective grip on a global scale, not just an individual scale. Until we do, we will continue to use the oppositional system of government that the ego loves. The separation is evident in the behavior of leaders in senates and parliaments across the globe which lack the cooperation and oneness that *awakening* brings.

The behavior in the halls of power reflects the ego at work. Their discussions are not about what will bring the greatest benefit to those whom they serve but about winning at any cost. That is the ego taking hold to ensure its power continues at a country and global level.

Your personal *awakening* will contribute to a global change.

Why has the world changed, why are we seeking more and why have we suddenly become more spiritual?

The entire planet has been moving towards *awakening* since time began. It is changing now that this movement is breaking free from the domination of the ego and its ways towards a more enlightened holistic view.

We have always been spiritual by nature because that is who we are. The ego says we are just seeking comfort in a world that has no meaning and that only weak minds need a god. The truth is we are consciousness having a human experience. One inspired by the ego. The ego always wishes to cover this up and keep the delusion going. The divine keeps calling us and we are emerging from the delusion.

It is clear we all share the planet and that its health is in our best interest. When war or disease strikes, it is in all our interest to respond. The view of the ego that we are separate is fading and the truth that we are all one is beginning to be seen.

When the two richest people on the planet give away most of their wealth, it is an indicator that the ego's insatiable thirst is no longer prepared to be quenched by all of us. Change is coming. Sanity will prevail. Governments will be next to change and the ego-centered way of "we must win" will fall to the heart-based way of "we must all win".

That will be the next shift that will occur. Your part in it is to *awaken*. Buddha said:

> *Imagine that every person in the world is enlightened but you. They are all your teachers, each doing just the right things to help you learn perfect patience, perfect wisdom, perfect compassion.(1)*

Once you embrace this as an experience, not a belief, it will not be forced; it will be a reality that can be no other way. Every day will be a teaching experience. Events will not be seen as random, disconnected things that occur. They will be known as part of an interconnected universe that is seeking to free you. The divine will always prompt you to take notice.

Every moment the divine is sending you messages to break through the illusion that the ego has constructed and call you back home to who you are. It cannot make you listen as that would take away your free will. However, as you begin to *awaken*, you will see every moment as a call to you. Many of you now hear that call, and that is why the world is slowly *awakening*.

Slowly each person is adjusting to the insanity that we witness every night on TV during the news. We all know the ego's way does not work. By each *awakening*, that world balance will shift and we will finally put down the weapons the ego loves and embrace the truth.

We are all one. Now is the time to *awaken*.

Your choice is to ignore it temporarily or to awaken now.

REFERENCES

1. Huxter, M, "A present centred awareness: a path to psychological freedom", www.buddhanet.net/present.htm.

2. Helliwell, J, Layard, R & Sachs, J (eds) 2013, *World happiness report 2013*, US Sustainable Development Solutions Network, New York, http://unsdsn.org/wp-content/uploads/2014/02/WorldHappinessReport2013_online.pdf.

3. New Economics Foundation, Happy Planet Index, www.happyplanetindex.org/data/.

4. Lao Tzu, *Tao Te Ching*.

5. JAXA, "The latest mystery of the universe", http://global.jaxa.jp/article/interview/vol22/p2_e.html

6. Schucman, H 1975, *A course in miracles*, Foundation for Inner Peace, Mill Valley, CA.

7. The English Standard Version Bible.

8. Hawking, S 1996, "The beginning of time", lecture, www.hawking.org.uk/the-beginning-of-time.html.

9. Ibarra, H 2015, "The authenticity paradox", *Harvard Business Review*, January–February, pp. 52–59.

10. www.goodreads.com/author/quotes/9810.Alb ert_Einstein; http://einstein.biz/quotes.php .

11. University of Virginia School of Medicine, The Division of Perpetual Studies, www.medicine.virginia.edu/clinical/departm ents/psychiatry/sections/cspp/dops/home-page.

12. *The Matrix* 1999, Warner Bros.

13. Tolle, E 1997, *The power of now: a guide to spiritual enlightenment*, Namaste Publishing, Vancouver, Canada.

14. Engel, P 2014, Map: Divorce rates around the world, Business Insider Australia, www.businessinsider.com.au/map-divorce-rates-around-the-world-2014-5.

15. *Śrī Brahma Samhitā* (2nd edn) 1985, Bhaktivedanta Book Trust, Alachua, FL.

16. "Meditation has 'some benefit against anxiety, depression and pain'", *Medical News Today*, 7 January 2014, www.medicalnewstoday.com/articles/270824. php.

17. For example, Kubler Ross, E 1969, *On death and dying: what the dying have to teach doctors, nurses, clergy and their own families*, Routledge, Abingdon, UK.

18. http://en.wikipedia.org/wiki/Observer_effect_%28physics%29.

19. http://en.wikipedia.org/wiki/Sumerian_creation_myth.

20. Begley, S & Wickham, C 2012, "A Nobel prize for being in two places at once", Reuters, 9 October, www.reuters.com/article/2012/10/09/us-nobel-physics-quantum-idUSBRE8980V620121009; and "Scientists prove that a particle can be in two places at once: everything gets weird" 2015, *HuffPost Tech*, 12 May, www.huffingtonpost.co.uk/2015/03/31/scientists-prove-that-a-particle-can-be-in-two-places-at-once_n_6975466.html.

21. Padmasambhava & Karma Linga 2013, *The Tibetan book of the dead: awakening upon dying*, E Guarisco & N Simmons (trans.), North Atlantic Books, Berkeley, CA.

22. Rinpoche, S 2009, *The Tibetan book of the living and dying*, rev. edn., HarperCollins, New York.

23. Goldberg, P 2013, "Spiritual but not religious: misunderstood and here to stay", *Huffington Post*, 13 February, www.huffingtonpost.com/philip-goldberg/spiritual-but-not-religious-misunderstood-and-here-to-stay_b_2617306.html.

The Teachings and RIM Training

For information on training in the practices, *Awaken* events or finding an RIM teacher, please contact us through the *Awaken* website.

Join the worldwide movement to *awaken* our world by *awakening* yourself.

www.awakenbook.com

All quotes from *A Course in Miracles* are from the 1975 edition ©Foundation for Inner Peace, P.O. Box 598, Mill Valley, 94942-0598, www.acim.org and info@acim.org.